LABOUR AND POVERTY IN
RURAL TANZANIA

The World Employment Programme (WEP) was launched by the International Labour Organisation in 1969, as the ILO's main contribution to the International Development Strategy for the Second United Nations Development Decade.

The means of action adopted by the WEP have included the following:

– short-term high-level advisory missions;
– longer-term national or regional employment teams; and
– a wide-ranging research programme.

Through these activities the ILO has been able to help national decision-makers to reshape their policies and plans with the aim of eradicating mass poverty and unemployment.

A landmark in the development of the WEP was the World Employment Conference of 1976, which proclaimed inter alia that 'strategies and national development plans should include as a priority objective the promotion of employment and the satisfaction of the basic needs of each country's population'. The Declaration of Principles and Programme of Action adopted by the Conference will remain the cornerstone of WEP technical assistance and research activities during the 1980s

This publication is the outcome of a WEP project.

LABOUR
AND
POVERTY
IN
RURAL TANZANIA

Ujamaa and Rural Development in the United Republic of Tanzania

PAUL COLLIER, SAMIR RADWAN,
and SAMUEL WANGWE,

with

ALBERT WAGNER

A study prepared for the
International Labour Office
within the framework of the
World Employment Programme

CLARENDON PRESS · OXFORD
1986

Oxford University Press, Walton Street, Oxford OX2 6DP

Oxford New York Toronto
Delhi Bombay Calcutta Madras Karachi
Kuala Lumpur Singapore Hong Kong Tokyo
Nairobi Dar es Salaam Cape Town
Melbourne Auckland

and associated companies in
Beirut Berlin Ibadan Nicosia

Oxford is a trade mark of Oxford University Press

Published in the United States
by Oxford University Press, New York

The designations employed in ILO publications, which are in conformity with United Nations
practice, and the presentation of material therein do not imply the expression of any opinion
whatsoever on the part of the International Labour Office concerning the legal status of any country,
area or territory or of its authorities, or concerning the delimitation of its frontiers.

The responsibility for opinions expressed in studies and other contributions rests solely with their
authors, and publication does not constitute an endorsement by the International Labour Office of
the opinions expressed in them.
Reference to names of firms and commercial products and processes does not imply their endorsement
by the International Labour Office, and any failure to mention a particular firm, commercial
product or process is not a sign of disapproval.

British Library Cataloguing in Publication Data

Collier, Paul
Labour and poverty in rural Tanzania:
Ujamaa and rural development.
1. Agriculture and state—Tanzania
I. Title II. Radwan, Samir III. Wange,
Samuel
338.1'8678 HD2128.5
ISBN 0–19–828531–0

Set by Spire Print Services, Salisbury
Printed in Great Britain at
the University Printing House, Oxford
by David Stanford
Printer to the University

CONTENTS

LIST OF TABLES

1

Tanzanian Rural Development: The Issues

Introduction

> But I am a very poor prophet. . . . In 1967 a group of youths who
> marched in support of the Arusha Declaration asked me how long
> it would take Tanzania to become socialist. I thought 30 years. I
> was wrong again: I am now sure that it will take us much longer!
>
> Julius K. Nyerere (1977)

The main objective of this study is to provide an up-to-date assessment of Tanzania's experience in rural development. Since the
Arusha Declaration of 1967, many writers have attempted such an
appraisal. There is a wealth of literature on various aspects of the
'Ujamaa' system; but most of this literature suffers from a lack of
hard data, as a result of which, arguments are couched in general-
izations supported by little empirical evidence. The starting-point of
this study is the emphasis laid by the Arusha Declaration on agriculture as 'the basis of development'. This is contrasted with President
Nyerere's candid admission that:

Ten years after the Arusha Declaration, Tanzania is certainly neither socialist, nor self-reliant. The nature of exploitation has changed, but it has not
been altogether eliminated. There are still great inequalities between citizens. Our democracy is imperfect. A life of poverty is still the experience of
the majority of our citizens.[1]

Our analysis is based on the results of the Household and Village
Survey carried out by the International Labour Office (ILO) and
the Department of Economics of Dar es Salaam University over the
period June–September 1980. The Survey covered a randomly
chosen sample of 600 households in twenty villages located in eight
different regions of the country. It provides a basis on which many of
the current controversies can at last be resolved empirically.

The evolution of policy

The Arusha Declaration inaugurated an era of major agricultural
policy interventions. These interventions were of an overtly political

nature (rather than being merely technical); indeed, 'Politics is Agriculture' became a central campaign slogan. The outcome of these interventions was a massive transformation of the rural areas between 1967 and 1980. Undoubtedly, the most visible manifestation of this transformation is the physical relocation of the bulk of the rural population from scattered individual settlements to government-planned villages. This intervention alone was so enormous that it is virtually without parallel in the rural development policies of any other country (with the possible exception of the *villages socialistes* in Algeria). However, during the same period, a whole array of other policies was implemented, covering communalization of production, the provision of social infrastructure, and the stimulation of agricultural output. These four sets of policies—namely, villagization, communalization, social infrastructure, and agricultural output—were distinct, though interrelated, interventions. They were distinct in that the Government's emphasis shifted from one to another very substantially over time as did accomplishments. They were interrelated both technically—for example, improved social infrastructure might assist efforts to raise agricultural output or might compete for resources with these efforts—and politically, for the concept of an Ujamaa village embraced all four. It was this political concept which captured the imagination and attention of outside observers.

The Ujamaa village concept evolved from the efforts of small groups of peasants in Tanga and Ruvuma during the early 1960s. The original concept was that the village would be an organization of poor peasants (that is, not including the upper peasantry), trying to raise their living standards by hard and disciplined communal work. The organization of production would copy that of capitalist plantations rather than peasant agriculture. Farming would be large scale and workers would be strictly supervised and disciplined. It was intended that communal production would be extended from agriculture to include a wide range of consumer goods and social services, eventually to the point at which private production activities would disappear.

Established during the optimism of the immediate post-Independence years, many of these settlements withered as the 1960s progressed so that by the end of the decade, von Freyhold estimates, there could not have been more than fifty surviving.[2]

It was at this stage that the Government decided to encourage and promote the formation of Ujamaa villages based on this set of principles. The instruments used by the Government were exhortation and the selective allocation of social infrastructure projects. The latter linked the Government's desire for Ujamaa with a second distinct but synchronized policy decision to improve rural social infrastructure by devoting to it a much increased budget allocation. This chosen method of stimulating the formation of Ujamaa villages by promising preferential allocations of social expenditure was a powerful and effective incentive. By 1973, around 10–15 per cent of the rural population had chosen to locate itself in such villages. However, in several crucial respects, the resulting villages differed from those established earlier. First, while the original Ujamaa villages had been composed of the poorer peasantry, the new villages included members of the upper peasantry keen to acquire improvements in social infrastructure but lacking an economic interest in communal production and distribution. Secondly, the motivation for Ujamaa shifted from a desire to improve living standards by collective productive effort, to a desire to become clients of government-provided social services. Thirdly, the attitudes underlying the social sanctions which sustain communal activity shifted from an understanding of the need for disciplined behaviour to a greater reliance upon altruism, or a more traditional 'uncalculating co-operativeness'.[3] Fourthly, the size of a village increased substantially from the very small original groupings—partly in response to a perceived need on the part of the Government to achieve economies of scale in its infrastructure projects.

One consequence of these differences was that the villages established in the period 1968–74 were not independent peasant organizations but dependent, centrally controlled organizations. This integration into central control was itself an objective of the Government, an objective not satisfied by the original Ujamaa settlements. As a result, although the Government encouraged the new villages, it disbanded most of the original Ujamaa schemes which had between them formed the Ruvuma Development Association.[4]

The villages established in response to government inducements adopted organizational structures laid down by the Government. The villagers elected a chairman, a secretary, and a treasurer, together with a council. These elected representatives also formed the membership of five village committees covering production, education, health, defence, and finance. In addition to the council, it

Labour and Poverty

was decided that a village assembly should be held at least once each year.

The Government also suggested a way of organizing communal labour. Overseers who would assign and supervise communal labour were to be elected. Work was to be allocated in the form of specific, measurable tasks to be accomplished in specified periods. That part of communal output which was distributed to village members was to be allocated in proportion to their labour input, which was to be monitored and recorded.

However, by the early 1970s, the priority which the Government attached to communalization of production was diminishing in relation to its priorities of village formation and social infrastructure. In 1972, the Government issued a directive permitting block farming in addition to communal farming. There were now three types of farming: purely individual, block farming, and communal. Block farming was supposed to combine individual initiative and the advantages of large-scale farming operations (e.g. clearing the land, tractorization). Certain cropping decisions were taken communally.

Nevertheless, by 1973 the Government found the pace of village formation, induced by preferential access to social facilities, to be too slow. Clearly, the Government could not afford to provide, on a national scale, a level of social facilities sufficient to induce the entire rural population to establish villages. As more villages were formed and the budgetary cost of services rose, the inducements had to be curtailed; and so the pace of voluntary village formation slowed (Table 1.1).

It was against this background that, in late 1973, the Government decided to abandon its strategy of voluntary inducements in favour of compulsion. Between May and December 1974, Operation Sogeza (Moving) implemented this decision so that by 1975 a large

Table 1.1: Number of registered Ujamaa villages

1969	809
1970	1 956
1971	4 484
1972	5 556
1973	5 628
1974 (Jan.)	5 008

Source: Coulson, *Tanzania: A political economy*, p. 241.

majority of the rural population was resident in villages. Sites for these villages had been hastily chosen by regional and district government administration. The criteria for choosing sites were that they should be on or near roads and have sufficient land to support at least 300 families—this number being the decreed legal minimum for a village.[5]

Communalization was not considered necessarily to be entailed in establishing the new villages. Indeed, the legislation which provided a legal entity for the new villages, the 1975 'Villages and Ujamaa Villages Act', made this quite clear. The villages established during 1974 were not necessarily Ujamaa villages. To have this legal status, certain levels of communal activity had to be achieved. Indeed, in a communiqué of January 1978 the Government announced that of the 7,400 villages in the United Republic of Tanzania none was Ujamaa.

Nevertheless, Tanzanian villages were not merely agglomerations of population. Collectively, the village organization had four functions to perform. First, the village was a unit for the provision of social infrastructure and was responsible for the establishment and maintenance of some of these services. Secondly, it was at least potentially a unit of communal production even though this had been given a low priority. Thirdly, it was empowered to allocate land among private cultivators, so that the village council could be an agency of land reform even without a communal sector. Fourthly, the village was the primary unit in the crop marketing chain. Though reforms of crop marketing in fact reduced their function to being nothing more than collection points, there was the potential for a more substantial role.

Although during the period 1968–72, communalization was a major objective, it clearly came second to villagization and the provision of social infrastructure during the period 1973–5. However, from 1975 the objective of agricultural production became of primary concern as several bad harvests and a sharp decline in the marketed surplus created a series of agricultural crises. The Government's response to these crises was to import food and to mount a succession of campaigns to raise output. The first of these, Operation Kilimo (Agriculture), was launched in December 1974. Peasants were exhorted to plant a minimum of three acres of food crops and one acre of cash crops, and to some extent exhortation shaded into compulsion as local bureaucrats attempted to meet the nationally determined objectives.

In 1978, the Government appointed 4,000 village managers to help plan and implement rural development projects. In part, this was a further indication of the Government's increasing concern with stimulating rural production. It also strengthened the capability of villages to plan for communal projects, although many managers had neither training nor experience for such a role. Potentially, the village manager and the village council together could design and implement communal activities. The essential institutional framework for communal activity was present. This is of some importance because the Government's commitment to the communalization of production had never been reversed, but had rather been relegated to a low priority. The achievement of villagization and the provision of a remarkable level of social infrastructure in rural areas—two objectives which had dominated the mid-1970s—were themselves similarly relegated in the 1980s owing to severe budgetary constraints leaving the way open for production growth and communalization to be given higher priority. During 1980 and 1981, the Tanzanian political leadership publicly renewed its old commitment to communalization. It was clear that unless there was a severe and insurmountable trade off between the objectives of communalization and growth in output, vigorous attempts would have to be made to give content to the bare framework.

Conclusions of earlier evaluation studies

Recently, various researchers have produced evaluations of Tanzanian rural development policy, with particular emphasis being placed upon the objective of communalization. von Freyhold, whose study is the major work on the subject, concludes that: 'Cooperation remained a short and unsatisfactory episode.'[6] Lofchie comes to a similar assessment: 'It is now generally acknowledged that Tanzania's policy of rural collectivization has been abandoned as a failure.'[7] Lofchie's statement is echoed almost verbatim by Ergos: 'It is now generally acknowledged that the policy of creating Ujamaa villages has failed.'[8] A similar statement is made by Putterman: 'The Government's promotion of collective agriculture has shown signs of general failure.'[9]

Those who wished to reach a different conclusion have tended to concede the assessment of the recent past but have at the same time argued that this is no guide to the future. A particularly clear statement of this position is that of Samoff, who suggests that researchers 'must have sufficient understanding of history not to be confused by the dramatic events of the moment'.[10]

The main explanations offered to account for the failure of communalism are in terms of a misplaced emphasis on government assistance to villages. The provision of social service infrastructure as a gift from the Government is considered to have made the peasants parasites.[11] What was needed was support for the poorer peasants against kulaks, bureaucrats, and arrogant technical staff who did not listen to peasant needs;[12] or, more particularly, support for the poorer peasants against the obstructionism of kulaks. Unfortunately, neither was forthcoming because 'to the administration, every peasant looked the same'.[13]

Communalism, however, was only one of several objectives of Tanzanian rural development policies. Many observers pointed to the achievements in the provision of social infrastructure as outstanding successes which improved the quality of rural life.[14] What the peasantry themselves thought about the changes in their quality of life is not known. In 1977 von Freyhold briefly revisited villages which she had studied in the early seventies and offered a depressing account of peasants' self-assessment: 'The period between 1971 and 1977 had been a time of stagnation or decline and the future looked rather unpromising.'[15] 'If they had ever believed in promises of a better future at Independence or during the Ujamaa campaign, they were no longer inclined to do so.'[16] But the most recent and comprehensive analysis of rural development policy, that of Coulson, returns an open verdict. Coulson concludes that 'villagization cannot be said to have failed . . . but the acid test is production over time'.[17] The verdict remains open not just in the sense of Samoff's observation that production might grow in the future, but because major uncertainties remain about what has happened to output during the decade of the seventies. At the macro-level the various agricultural output series differ to quite an astonishing extent concerning both levels and trends. At the micro-level there have been very few quantitative studies based on villages. It is in this data vacuum that research assessments fall back upon statements of the form 'It is now generally acknowledged that . . .'.

A major effort has gone into the analysis of that part of the macro-agricultural data which is reasonably reliable, namely output marketed through official channels. Studying the period 1970–80, and smoothing out transient variations due to climate, Ellis finds a dramatic deterioration in the barter terms of trade for peasant agriculture of the order of 36 per cent over the decade.[18] The income terms of trade deteriorated by a staggering 33 per cent which, as Ellis comments, was 'incompatible with rising rural living standards' and 'incompatible with the realization of sustained increases in agricultural productivity'.[19] This macro-data, however, is an imperfect guide to peasant incomes because it omits subsistence output, unofficial crop marketings, and non-crop sources of income. More important, it tells us little about the distribution of peasant income or about processes of income generation. Indeed, the literature on Tanzanian rural development has brought forth a series of important issues and hypotheses which quite simply cannot be answered without quantitative data at the micro-level. We now turn to the identification of these unresolved issues to which our own survey data may then be addressed.

Unresolved issues

Rural inequality

One of the principal motivating factors behind the original foundation of Ujamaa villages was the desire to eliminate perceived vast inequalities among the Tanzanian peasantry.[20] Indeed, if the Ujamaa programme has remained largely unimplemented this may mean that large inequalities among the peasantry persist. If so, given that about 85 per cent of Tanzanians live in villages, intra-rural inequality would clearly be the major contributor to overall inequality in Tanzania. Yet commentaries on inequality in the country have focused almost exclusively on the other two components of inequality, intra-urban inequality and rural-urban income differences. For example, many articles cite the differentials among urban wage-earners without acknowledging that this component of inequality is quite peripheral to overall inequality. Wage and salary employment constituted only 8.1 per cent of the estimated labour force in 1982, according to the Ministry of Manpower Development and Administration in Dar es Salaam.

Inequality in rural areas is also of vital importance because of its connection with poverty. As in most African economies, the poor are concentrated in rural areas and poverty can be regarded primarily as a rural phenomenon. Although the comparison of rural and urban living standards is problematic, the few African case studies concur in finding a higher incidence of poverty in rural than in urban areas.[21] Thus, whereas around 85 per cent of the population is rural, an even greater percentage of the poor live in rural areas. Yet the greater the extent of inequality in rural areas the less correct it would be to treat the poor and the rural population as synonymous. Where there is considerable inequality, measures which do indeed raise mean rural incomes can nevertheless have quite perverse effects upon the poor. It was the perception of this problem which prompted the Government to depart from its immediate post-Independence agricultural strategies.

Finally, intra-rural inequality is of importance because it is claimed that it is the upper peasantry which has acquired power within the organizational structures of villages. Further, it is alleged that this group is behaving as an élite which, perceiving its interests to be threatened by communalization, has succeeded in defeating the early efforts to achieve that objective. von Freyhold, Putterman, and Coulson all advance propositions along these lines.

The above considerations establish the central importance of intra-rural inequality. Yet, previous work has not advanced much beyond theorizing on the role of kulaks and anecdotal evidence of income differentiation and the concentration of power. There are four major tasks concerning the analysis of inequality which must be carried out, provided that relevant micro-data exist. First, the extent of rural inequality must be established. Is it indeed the case that there are 'vast inequalities' as asserted by Ergos,[22] von Freyhold,[23] Shivji,[24] and Raikes,[25] or do 'all peasants look the same'?

This is quite a demanding task because while peasant incomes are generally low in absolute terms, their structure is highly complex. Observed inequalities may in fact be the spurious product of inappropriate measurement. The passage from anecdotal to statistical evidence will therefore involve first, not just the collection of an appropriate set of data (daunting as that task is in the context of the rural areas of Tanzania), but a methodological inquiry into welfare-based concepts of peasant income.

Secondly, the observed extent of rural inequality can be broken down into various components. Fundamental to the whole programme of villagization is the extent to which inequalities are found mainly within villages or between them. Some observers have linked the major inequalities within the rural areas to differences in ecology between regions. If this is indeed the case then initiatives at the village level to reduce inequality are largely impotent. The village council is an organization with the potential to alter income distribution within the village by means of communalization or land reallocation. Yet if inequalities are primarily between—rather than within—villages, then policy initiatives must be formulated centrally, at the national level, rather than locally, at the village level. The political issue of the centralization or decentralization of power has been a dominant one in post-Arusha Tanzania and policy in this respect is still in a state of flux. Several commentators have criticized the Government for over-centralizing and denuding village organizations of real power. Yet these criticisms appear to encounter a dilemma. If inequalities are mainly between villages, a decentralized power structure will not be capable of reducing rural inequality. On the other hand, if large inequalities within villages predominate, and if the upper peasantry has indeed seized control of the village power structure (a hypothesis which we have outlined above), then a decentralized power structure of this type will still be powerless to reduce inequality.

It would be difficult to over-stress the importance of this issue for Tanzanian rural development. Most explanations offered by commentators for the perceived lack of success in rural development programmes to date, come down to criticism of the existing centralized control system as remote, bureaucratic, and ill-informed. If such criticisms are well founded, then they lead to the conclusion that a centralized decision structure for rural development in the present circumstances of Tanzania will be inherently unsuited for implementing an effective egalitarian programme. Yet the alternative—a decentralized decision structure—which the Government has not to date really attempted, would probably also fail to implement such a programme unless there were a conjunction of two circumstances: (*a*) existing inequalities must be located primarily within rather than between villages; and (*b*) power must be diffused among all levels of village society rather than captured by the upper peasantry. Given the present structure of Tanzanian institutions these two conditions would appear to be jointly necessary for egalitarian rural development to have a chance of success, even if the Government were prepared to implement a policy of decentralization. Whether either or both of these two conditions are in fact met is an empirical question which we will investigate below. An affirmative answer would support a policy of decentralization to the village level authorities; a negative answer would lead to the depressing conclusion that methods which did not succeed in the past must somehow be made to work in the future.

The final task in our analysis of inequality is the most substantial. The investigations outlined above have sought to analyse and measure inequality and to correlate it with power at the village level. However, it is also necessary to attempt to explain inequalities of income in terms of other variables. The relevance of such an analysis for policy is obvious. Given that the administrative infrastructure and taxation system are inadequate to bring about substantial direct transfers of income in rural Tanzania, inequality can only be reduced by tackling its causes. Yet, inequality might arise for a variety of reasons. For example, we might find that poor rural households have low incomes because they use available resources less effectively than other households. If this is the case then there may well be a trade-off between the Government's objectives of equity and output growth, for extra resources given to the poor will be less productive than if given to the upper peasantry. Moreover, it would suggest that an egalitarian development programme should concentrate upon advising and informing poor peasants on how to alter farming practices.

Alternatively, some peasants may be poor, not because they use their resources inefficiently, but because they have few resources to use. The policy implications will in this case depend upon which resources the poor lack. If, for example, most poor households have low incomes because they have less labour than other households, the scope for successful intervention may be rather limited. A poor widow may not be greatly helped by receiving enlarged supplies of fertilizer. Rather, some attempt must be made to provide her with direct and recurrent transfers of income. Such transfers pose considerable budgetary and administrative problems, which are likely to be prohibitive at Tanzania's level of development.

Only if rural inequality is found to be caused by differential endowments of resources other than labour is effective egalitarian policy intervention likely to be successful. Moves to reallocate non-labour resources from richer to poorer peasant households are administratively and financially feasible in Tanzania, whereas recurrent income transfers are probably not. Furthermore, if differ-

ences in income are explained by differences in resource endowments rather than inefficiency of utilization, then such reallocations
would not conflict with the pressing objective of raising agricultural
output.

The explanation of inequality, which will enable us to discover
which of the above hypotheses is applicable to rural Tanzania, is a
daunting task. However, before inequality can be explained an
explanation of income is necessary, and because the sources of
peasant income are diverse this involves a series of attempts to
discover the determinants of particular income components. Thus,
the analysis of why peasant incomes differ becomes the core of our
study.

We have suggested above that under certain conditions the transfer of non-labour resources among rural households may be a feasible and desirable instrument of Tanzanian rural development policy. The villagization policy which has already been implemented
may to some extent have achieved such a reallocation. In particular,
villagization generally (though not always) involves households
abandoning their existing landholdings and being allocated new
holdings by the village council. We have already noted that the
village council was the legal entity in which land rights were vested,
so that it had the potential to effect any redistribution of land which
it regarded as desirable. Whether villagization did in fact produce
land reform is not known, owing to the paucity of data on landholdings either before or after Operation Sogeza. Some commentators,
however, have cast doubt upon the extent of actual land redistribution. Putterman suggests that private claims to land have in practice
been protected by being socially acceptable locally, despite the legal
prerogative of the village council.[26] De Vries and Fortmann go
further and suggest that in some instances villagization might have
actually accentuated land shortage because some villages were
badly situated in areas where there was little usable land, and
because the relatively large concentrations of population in villages
led to a reduction in average plot size to offset the increase in distance between dwellings and farms.[27] Our study is able to proceed
further towards resolving both these issues by comparing the holdings which individual households operated before Operation Sogeza
with those currently operated. By reducing sampling error, this
offers a degree of accuracy which could not be attained by comparing sample survey distributions at different dates, even if such data
were ever to become available.

We shall now review the hypotheses concerning inequality which are currently unresolved, together with their implications for policy. Our starting-point is to discover the extent of inequalities and thus to decide between earlier hypotheses:

 (i) the Tanzanian peasantry is characterized by vast inequalities, or
 (ii) all peasants look alike.

If hypothesis (i) is found to hold then the decomposition of inequality becomes an issue. Again we must distinguish between two hypotheses:

 (iii) most rural inequality arises out of differences between villages, or
 (iv) most rural inequality arises out of differences within villages.

If (iii) holds, then a centralized rural development programme is logically necessary to achieve an egalitarian outcome. If (iv) holds then village-level decision-taking may be more desirable, depending upon whether or not the upper peasantry dominates the village organs of potential power. Testable hypotheses follow:

 (v) village organizations are dominated by the upper peasantry, or
 (vi) representation in village organizations is widely diffused among social groups.

If (v) holds, then a centralized power structure is politically necessary to achieve egalitarian objectives even if (iv) holds. Alternatively a truly democratic decentralized organization which would facilitate the allocation of power to the majority of peasants would be capable of handling this problem. If both (vi) and (iv) hold, however, the case for decentralization is strong. In the Tanzanian context decentralization is a concept which is normally used to represent the reallocation of power to the regions, as opposed to centralization, representing power located in the capital. Therefore, we need to distinguish between the decentralization of power to village level (as used here) and decentralization to the regional administration (as in official usage).

In this context, therefore, the problem ceases to be seen in terms of two alternatives, i.e. centralization or decentralization (to village level). A third possibility emerges, namely decentralization to regional level. The significance of this third level will depend on the degree to which inequality between villages is a reflection of inequalities between regions. If village inequalities derive from regional inequalities, then there is a strong case for centralization. If not, then there is a strong case for decentralization to the regions which can then deal with village inequalities. This distinction has important implications for policy with respect to the degree or level of decentralization.

Deciding between the first two hypotheses determines whether rural inequality should be on the policy agenda. Choosing among the next four hypotheses offers a guide to the appropriate level of agency for policy formulation. The remaining issues concern which policy instruments would be appropriate for agencies to adopt. The choice from among these depends upon which of a number of possible explanations of inequality is the most accurate.

(vii) Inequalities reflect differences in efficiency of resource utilization, or

(viii) inequalities reflect differences in possession of resources.

If (vii) holds, egalitarian development may have to be curtailed as output requirements become pressing. If (viii) holds, then the issue becomes whether inequality is the result of differences in labour or non-labour resources:

(ix) inequalities reflect different endowments of household labour, or

(x) inequalities reflect different endowments of non-labour resources.

If (ix) holds, then policy agencies face the daunting task of designing and implementing some system of transfer payments. If (x) holds, agencies should attempt the relatively easier task of reallocating assets. The question which then naturally arises is the extent to which this has already happened.

(xi) Villagization has achieved a significantly more egalitarian land allocation, or

(xii) villagization has not altered land distribution.

Finally, if (xi) holds, we may ask whether or not this has been at the price of reduced holding sizes:

(xiii) mean plot size was unaltered or increased by Operation Sogeza, or

(xiv) mean plot size was reduced by Operation Sogeza.

The above discussion establishes our agenda for investigating rural inequality. We now turn to certain unresolved issues relating to the provision of social infrastructure.

The provision of social infrastructure

There is little dispute about the extent of provision of social infra-structure in the rural areas. In three distinct areas—basic health facilities, adult literacy, and primary education—the Government has succeeded in implementing major programmes of improved provision.

In the provision of health facilities, there was a shift in emphasis away from urban hospitals towards rural health centres and dispensaries. The share of the national health budget devoted to urban hospitals fell from 73 per cent at the beginning of the 1970s to 60 per cent by 1979. The population per health centre fell from 234,000 in 1969 to 83,000 in 1979, the population per dispensary falling from 8,100 to 6,700 during the same period. Rather surprisingly, the national data suggest that this improved availability did not lead to a substantial increase in use of health facilities, the number of out-patient visits per person per year being no higher in 1978 than in 1972. This, however, might well have been because people visited facilities at an earlier stage of illness and so required less treatment. There is, of course, no clear correlation between visits to health facilities and the state of health of the rural population.

The achievements in respect of adult literacy have been among the most impressive in the world. National data indicate that by 1977, adult illiteracy had fallen to only 27 per cent of the population, this being far below the illiteracy rate in many countries with con-siderably higher per capita GNP. A similar effort has been made to expand primary education. On a national scale, some 70 per cent of children in the official primary school age range were attending school by 1980 (UNESCO, *Statistical Yearbook, 1983*, Table 3.2, p. III–32).

Though the extent of social provision is known from macro-data such as these, other important aspects remain uncertain. First, little is known about the differential access to facilities within rural areas.

Recent studies in other developing countries have found that utilization of health and education facilities, in particular, is quite strongly biased against the poorer sections of the rural population.[28]

This form of inequality might come about in rural Tanzania if certain villages were generally favoured with government facilities. In particular, villages with successful agriculture and thus relatively higher incomes might attract a disproportionate share of public funds. In addition, inequalities could occur within villages if the upper peasantry has a greater propensity to make use of modern facilities such as schools and health centres. This might arise because they are better able to afford the time, have a greater appreciation of the advantages, or are socially more at ease with the schoolteachers and health workers who dispense these benefits. We are able to use our survey data to investigate how the utilization of various facilities is distributed. Within the limits determined by our sample size, both the possibility of intra-village differentiation and that of favoured villages can be resolved.

It remains to consider the effects of social infrastructure provision. The ultimate aim of providing health facilities, for example, is not to treat the sick but rather to have a healthy population. Similarly, the provision of education and literacy may raise peasants' incomes by making them more productive. The investigation of whether these potential effects have actually been achieved is still in its infancy and only limited work has been carried out with reference to Africa. Our survey data, although they represent a considerable advance on what was previously available, can only begin to approach these issues. The measurement of health and the treatment of illness ideally require a level of specialist knowledge and detail which was beyond our resources. Nevertheless, with certain limitations, we are able to make an attempt at exploring these issues. In particular, we provide an estimate of the productive effects of education and literacy.

Communal production

The final set of unresolved issues on which we focus relates to attempts to communalize various elements of rural production, of which the most important to date has been crop output. The attractions of communal production relative to peasant production are threefold. First, it is more likely to produce an equitable distribution of income, although this depends upon the criteria which determine the distribution of communal output. Secondly, it enables certain economies of scale, such as insurance against risk.[29] Provided that there are no offsetting costs, this can potentially raise the level of agricultural output. Thirdly, because communal output is centralized, agricultural taxation, either on the part of the Government or by the village council itself, is made easier. Potentially, this enables peasants both greater expenditure upon social infrastructure and a higher savings rate.

However, against the communalization of agricultural production being successful there are severe drawbacks. Since Tanzanian peasants have limited experience of large-scale agricultural production (except, perhaps, by working as labourers on plantations) they will be confronted by an entirely new set of problems. Questions of what crops to plant, the phasing of work through the year, the labour intensity of cultivation, and the optimal use of inputs all require an explicit process of information-gathering and decision-taking quite unlike peasant choice-making.

In addition to being plunged into an unknown range of the production function, communalization raises problems of appropriate incentive structures. Since little of the traditional, pre-colonial *Ujamaa* (co-operation) remains, communal activity requires the conscious support of participating peasants. Such support will only be forthcoming if it is in the immediate interest of each participant. Putterman has recently shown that within a framework of household-choice theory, it is possible to construct an incentive structure for collective agriculture which is compatible with productive efficiency.[30] The efficient incentive structure is one in which the surplus value is retained or distributed by the village council, while the remainder of output (that part which is attributable to labour) is distributed to those who have worked on the communal farm, in proportion to the amount of work which each has contributed.

The circumstances under which communal production is voluntarily chosen by peasants are, in part, the conditions required for such an incentive structure to operate. The first such condition is that the communal labour input of each participant be measured and recorded. In the absence of this, distribution cannot be based upon work contribution. As we have seen, the structure of organization within Tanzanian villages has the potential to provide for such monitoring. However, several commentators have expressed doubts as to the technical book-keeping capability at the village level and the motivation to organize the distribution of communal output in this manner. Indeed Coulson has suggested that, because of low communal output, the authorities actually discouraged any distributions so as to avoid the appearance that returns to labour input were low.[31] For this reason, the first empirical issue addressed by our survey data on communal production is the extent of and the basis for the distribution of communal output.

Beyond the incentive system, determined by the basis for distribution of output, is the degree of communal spirit which motivates participants. A critical element of this spirit is the extent to which participants see the quantity of their labour contributions as being interdependent. Individuals can be expected to work harder if they feel their own efforts will be reciprocated by others in the group. Putterman has suggested that both this perception of reciprocity and the ability to monitor labour input will be stronger the smaller the communal group.

The remaining influence upon the extent of voluntary participation in communal agriculture is the relative productivity of labour in communal farming and in peasant farming. It is possible that there is sufficient surplus labour in villages for communal labour contributions not to compete with peasant agriculture. Whether labour utilization in peasant agriculture is so low as to produce a labour surplus will therefore be investigated through our survey data. If there is no observable labour surplus, then some estimate of relative labour productivity is required. Several commentators have made qualitative or quantitative assessments. von Freyhold describes the low quality of communal work and suggests that incomes in Ujamaa villages are invariably below those of peasant agriculture.[32] These views are echoed by Coulson and Ergos. Against this, Putterman has found that in two of the villages which he studied, average labour productivity was higher in communal agriculture than in peasant agriculture. It is therefore necessary to resolve this important issue.

The combination of labour productivity and the quantity of labour devoted to communal production determines total communal output. Using our own survey data together with recent government statistics collected from some 4,000 villages, we are able to estimate both total and relative communal output. The contribution made to date by communal agriculture to the objective of stimulating total agricultural production can thus be assessed.

Perhaps more important than the impact of communal agriculture upon total output are its consequences for income distribution. The communal *shamba* (farm) constitutes the village-level unit of taxation and expenditure, with individuals being taxed by way of contributions of communal labour. Expenditure is both payments for that labour at a common wage rate, and the provision of such infrastructure as the village council determines. Little attention has been paid to these distributional considerations, though Putterman found a tendency for households with more land and wealth to do less communal work.[33] However, since this result was not statistically significant, the issue of the relationship between household income and communal work needs further investigation. If Putterman's findings are indeed established, the possibility is raised that, as presently constituted, communal agriculture may be distributionally regressive.

Finally, we will investigate differences in communal production between villages in an attempt to test some of the hypothesized conditions for success. Are larger villages less successful at devoting resources productively to communal agriculture? Does the incentive system really matter? Is the mean private household income level in a village correlated with the level of communal activity? Other important hypothesized conditions cannot be investigated by means of our data. For example, the extent of communal motivation and perceptions of the interdependence of labour contributions are surely best approached through the techniques of social anthropology rather than questionnaire-based surveys. Nevertheless, we can proceed towards resolving major questions relating to communal production. As we have suggested, this may be important since communalization is likely to be back on the political agenda for the 1980s.

Notes

1. J. Nyerere, *The Arusha Declaration Ten Years After* (Dar es Salaam, Government Printer, 1977).
2. M. von Freyhold, *Ujamaa Villages in Tanzania: Analysis of a Social Experiment* (London, Heinemann, 1979), p. 73.
3. Ibid., p. 81.
4. See A. Coulson, *Tanzania: A Political Economy* (Oxford, Clarendon Press, 1982).
5. J. de Vries and L. P. Fortmann, 'Large scale villagization: Operation

Sogeza in Iringa Region', in A. Coulson (ed.), *African Socialism in Practice* (Nottingham, Spokesman, 1979), p. 129.

6. von Freyhold, op. cit.

7. M. F. Lofchie: 'Agrarian crisis and economic liberalisation in Tanzania', *Journal of Modern African Studies*, 16, 1978.

8. Z. Ergos: 'Why did the Ujamaa village policy fail?', *Journal of Modern African Studies*, 18, 1980, p. 387.

9. L. Putterman: 'Is a democratic collective agriculture possible?', *Journal of Development Economics*, 9, 1981, p. 375.

10. J. Samoff, 'Crises and socialism in Tanzania', *Journal of Modern African Studies*, 19, 1981, p. 306.

11. von Freyhold, op. cit., p. 103.

12. Ibid., p. 117.

13. Ibid., p. 86.

14. See in particular A. K. Sen, 'Public action and the quality of life in developing countries', *Oxford Bulletin of Economics and Statistics*, 43, 1981.

15. von Freyhold, op. cit., p. 187.

16. Ibid., p. 191.

17. Coulson, op. cit., pp. 261–2.

18. F. Ellis: 'Agricultural price policy in Tanzania', *World Development*, 10, 1982, pp. 263–83.

19. Ibid., p. 274.

20. von Freyhold, op. cit., p. 74.

21. On the measurement of rural and urban living standards see P. Collier and R. H. Sabot, 'Measuring the Difference between Rural and Urban Incomes', in R. H. Sabot (ed.), *Migration and the Labor Market in Developing Countries* (Boulder, Westview, 1982). Two studies of Kenya which, using different poverty lines, both find a higher rural incidence of poverty are E. Crawford and E. Thorbecke, *Employment, Income Distribution and Basic Needs in Kenya*, Report of an ILO Mission, mimeo (Cornell University, 1978) and P. Collier and D. Lal, 'Poverty and Growth in Kenya', Staff Working Paper 389 (Washington DC, World Bank, 1980).

22. Ergos, op. cit., p. 388.

23. von Freyhold, op. cit., p. 74.

24. I. G. Shivji, *Class Struggles in Tanzania* (London, Heinemann, 1976).

25. P. Raikes, 'Rural differentiation and class formation in Tanzania', *Journal of Peasant Studies*, 3, 1978, pp. 285–325.

26. Putterman, op. cit., p. 391.

27. de Vries and Fortmann, op. cit., pp. 129–32.

28. J. Meerman, *Public Expenditure in Malaysia: Who Benefits and Why?* (New York, Oxford University Press, 1979).

29. An excellent account of the production scale economies of communalization is given in von Freyhold, op. cit., pp. 22–8.

30. Putterman, op. cit., p. 385. The original theoretical formulation is by A. K. Sen: 'Labour allocation in a cooperative enterprise', *Review of Economic Studies*, 33, 1966, pp. 361–71.
31. Coulson, op. cit., p. 245.
32. von Freyhold, op. cit., pp. 84–5, 91, 107.
33. Putterman, op. cit., Table 2.

2

The Household and Village Survey

The only analysed budget survey giving national coverage of the rural areas of Tanzania is the 1969 Budget Survey of the Central Bureau of Statistics.[1] This is subject to two severe limitations. First, although it provides considerable data on consumption and income, the survey includes little information on labour use and none on land ownership. Second, it predates the major institutional changes which have taken place in the rural areas in the wake of the Arusha Declaration and so provides no guide as to the current level or distribution of rural income. Yet it is precisely because of these changes that the need for data is urgent.

The sample

The logistics of survey work in the rural areas are such as to place severe constraints upon what is feasible. A large sample size, apart from increasing expense, is purchased at the price of a severe decline in the ability to motivate and supervise enumerators with a consequent deterioration in the quality of data. Against this a small sample size necessitates either taking a small sample within each village—which undermines the study of intra-village differentiation—or inadequately covering ecological diversity. In the face of the type of environment found in Tanzania, the final choice reflects a compromise between these disadvantages. A stratified random sample was selected in the following manner. First, of the twenty regions in Tanzania, eight were selected according to type of cropping and farming so as to cover a wide spectrum of regional variations such as coastal, mountain cropping, mixed farming, and pastoral regions. A ninth region which we would have liked to include, Rukwa, was dropped owing to the difficulty of transport. The second step was to select districts within regions in such a way as to ensure coverage of the major agro-ecological zones of Tanzania. For this purpose, the Conyers Classification of the agro-economic zones of Tanzania was used to choose the eighteen different districts included in the sample.[2] The third step was to choose villages within each district.

Twenty villages were selected as randomly as possible, given certain constraints such as the availability of transport. A number of villages had to be rejected because of the difficulty of getting there. Nevertheless, the survey was by no means confined to easily accessible villages. Enumerators had to walk up to sixteen miles to reach selected villages. Finally, thirty households in each village were selected randomly either from the village list if it existed, or by first compiling a list of village inhabitants and picking the sample from there. The final sample thus consisted of 600 households in twenty villages. The total population of the sampled households was 3,200, this being 6 per cent of the total population of the surveyed villages (50,000). Table 2.1 provides a summary view of the sample structure, and Map 1 indicates the location of the villages selected.

It should at once be apparent that the resulting sample is insufficient for many inferences to be made at the national level. Our coverage of some 3,200 rural dwellers is in numerical terms inadequate as a guide to the circumstances of the 14 m. (1978) rural Tanzanians. However, the selection of regions and villages is regarded by experienced Tanzanians as being fairly representative, careful enumeration secured a response rate of usable questionnaires of 99 per cent, and at certain points where the survey data can be checked against reasonably reliable macro-data, the correspondence is reassuring.

The design of questionnaires

The survey applied three questionnaires which were the result of pilot testing earlier versions:

(*a*) the household questionnaire, which included questions on household characteristics, employment and labour use, emigration, ownership of land and other assets, sources of income, production, communal production, basic needs, and participation;

(*b*) the village questionnaire designed to provide data on the village history and economy, resource base, organization, services, and performance: this was essential in view of the importance of the village as a unit of planning and government policy;

(*c*) a project questionnaire, to collect data on the different projects in the village for the purpose of project appraisal in the different villages surveyed.

Table 2.1: Agro-ecological characteristics of regions, districts, and villages in the sample[a]

Region	District	Village	Zone	Rainfall (mm p. a.)
Tanga	Handeni	Kwaluguru	Highlands	700–1 500
	Lushoto	Kwemakame	Mountain area	800–2 000
	Tanga	Kichangani	Coastal	1 100–1 400
	Muheza	Gombelo	Coastal	900–1 300
	Korogwe	Kwakombo	Eastern cotton belt	800–1 000
Dodoma	Dodoma	Mvumi Mission	Dry cattle	500–650
	Dodoma	Chilonwa	Dry cattle	550–650
	Dodoma	Chiguluka	Dry cattle	550–650
	Kondoa	Mondo	Semi-pastoral	500–600
	Mpwapwa	Kisokwe	Highlands	650–800
Arusha	Arusha	Mareu	Plains	400–700
	Monduli	Manyara	Semi-pastoral	600–1 000
	Hanang	Nangara	Highlands	700–1 000
Kagera	Bukoba	Rwazi	Coffee highlands	1 100–2 000
	Muleba	Kamachumu	Coffee highlands	1 100–2 000
	Karagwe	Bugene	Highlands	800–900
Morogoro	Morogoro	Mlali	Cotton belt (plains)	700–1 000
Coast/Pwani	Kisarawe	Sungwi	Coastal hinterland (cashew)	900–2 000
Iringa	Iringa	Lulanzi	Woodlands (tobacco)	600–1 000
Mbeya	Mbeya	Iwala	Plains	400–600

[a]Agro-ecological characteristics as reported in Conyers: 'Agro-economic zones of Tanzania',

A guide to the analysis

As discussed in Chapter 1, the main purpose of the survey was to provide an empirical basis for assessing the performance of Tanzania's strategies for rural development. Thus, the analysis starts at the basic unit, the household. Chapter 3 provides household profiles in terms of demographic characteristics, employment structure and labour allocation, access to assets and to services, and income distribution. The main objective here is to paint a broad picture of various aspects of the standards of living and employment patterns found among the households, and to try to establish the inter-relationships that may exist between these aspects.

Chapter 4 provides the core of the analysis. Here the traditional mode of analysis based on the poverty datum line is abandoned, since it is judged as being of limited relevance to Tanzania, which is

Tsetse infestation	Population density	Land availability	Cattle ownership	Nearest town	Communications
—	Very low	Plenty	Medium/low	—	Poor
—	Dense/very dense	Shortage	Medium/low	District	Poor
—	Dense	Adequate		Regional	Good
—	Medium/dense	Plenty	Low	Regional	Good
—	Medium/dense	Adequate	Very low	—	Good
—	Medium/dense	Adequate	High	Regional	Good
—	Very low	Plenty	High	—	Average
—	Low/medium	Adequate	High	—	Good
Moderate	Medium/low	Plenty	Low	—	Average
—	Low	Adequate	Low	District	Average
—	Low	Adequate	High	—	Average
—	Medium	Plenty	Medium	—	Good
—	Medium	Adequate	High	District	Good
—	Very dense	Shortage	Low	Regional	Average
—	Very dense	Shortage	Low	Regional	Average
Moderate	Low/very low	Plenty	Medium	District	Poor
Moderate	Medium/low	Plenty	—	Regional	Good
Moderate	Medium/low	Plenty	—	District	Good
—	Medium	Plenty	Low	Regional	Good
Moderate	Very low	Plenty	High	—	Poor

Bralup Research Paper No. 25 (University of Dar es Salaam, 1978).

characterized by the preponderance of poor subsistence peasants. Under such conditions the quantification of poverty assumes secondary importance. More important are questions related to the attributes of poverty and the mechanisms that perpetuate poverty and inequality. Thus, the population was divided into two halves: the poor and the non-poor, according to whether the household incomes were below or above the median household income for the sample as a whole. This procedure is admittedly arbitrary. But the crucial questions investigated were what are the correlates of poverty and the causes of differentiation in the Tanzanian village. This analysis was done at three levels:

(*a*) By type of income: here data on income, labour use, asset distribution, and production are used to answer such questions as whether a low total income per household reflects a shortfall in one

Map 1: Tanzania. Rural Household and Village Survey: Village Sample

particular source of income, say sale of crop, or results from a low level of income from all sources; whether low income in a particular activity is caused by low prices or by low output, and whether low output in an activity is caused by a low input of endowments (land, livestock, skill, . . .) or a low return on these endowments.

(*b*) By endowments: here the impact of endowments on income differentials is explored, with endowments broadly defined to include labour, education, skills, and assets. The basic question here is whether low total income reflects a shortfall in particular endowments (labour force in the household, landholding, . . .) or a low return on these endowments (low wages, low yields, . . .). If the latter is true, i.e. returns are low, this can be broken down into:

(i) misallocation of endowments between activities;
(ii) lower returns on endowments within activities.

(*c*) At the third level of analysis, poverty is explained in terms of low prices for produce, a shortfall in particular endowments, misallocation of endowments, and low returns on endowments in particular activities. Each of these is in turn investigated in terms of other characteristics. For example, are low prices explicable in terms of low assets (suggesting an inability to store output to be sold when time offers favourable prices), or in terms of location? Is a low labour endowment explicable in terms of disability, or past out-migration?

In Chapter 5 the focus is on the village. Here an attempt is made to assess the performance of the village and explain inter-village differences. This part thus begins by depicting profiles of the twenty villages in terms of the facilities and social infrastructure (in the fields of health and education), as well as the institutional framework for participation. The question posed is whether villages which are well off tend to have better participation. This is followed by an analysis of the village economy. Two issues are discussed: first, the resource-base of the village and how resource-availability accounts for inter-village differentials; and second, the significance and contribution of communal activities (farm and non-farm) to the village economy. Finally, it is asked whether there are favoured villages, and if so, what are the reasons: resource endowments, higher skills, closeness to markets, cropping patterns, or some other variable.

The concluding chapter sums up the evidence. More specifically, it tries to pull together the major themes that have emerged from the previous analysis in an attempt to answer the question of whether the policies of Ujamaa and villagization have succeeded in achieving their objectives, namely, equitable distribution of wealth and income, introduction of the value of communal work, and efficiency of production.

Notes

1. The 1976/77 Survey results are just being made available but are not yet published.
2. D. Conyers, 'Agro-economic zones of Tanzania', in *Bralup Research Paper No. 25* (University of Dar es Salaam, 1978).

3

A Profile of the Village Household

In this chapter the survey data are used to construct a profile of village households in 1980. We begin with some basic demographic characteristics of households, such as their size and age structures, and their levels of education and health. Household membership is fluid owing to migration, with people leaving for towns or other villages and sometimes returning to their original household. The pattern of migration from rural households, about which not much is known, is therefore our second area of study. From the household, we then narrow our focus on to the labour force, describing the occupational profile and how labour time is split between various types of work. Non-labour household resources are then considered. The most important of these in Tanzanian peasant households are land and livestock. Finally, the composition of peasant production and income is constructed and the results compared with data from other sources to get an indication of the reliability of our findings.

Demographic characteristics

The concept of a peasant household is not straightforward, for its definition involves spatial, temporal, and economic aspects. For example, it greatly increases the reliability of our measurements if we confine membership of the household to those actually living together at the time of enumeration. However, this is unlikely to be how the household's members view the household. Some 'members' will be living elsewhere, perhaps temporarily, and some people present may be regarded as guests rather than members. Moreover, 'living together' is a flexible notion, which could involve sleeping under the same roof, or in the same compound, or sharing meals together, or having a particular kinship relationship. Different definitions of the household will affect the accuracy of the data and will also change the membership of the household. This in turn will affect the extent of measured inequalities of income between households, to take a particularly important example. In our survey a household was defined as people currently living together (sleeping under the same roof or in the same compound), including guests who had been present for more than two weeks. This definition produced a mean household size of 5.3 persons. We can check this against the findings of a nationwide survey which was conducted by the Central Bureau of Statistics in Tanzania in 1975. This survey, the 1975 Pilot Household Budget Survey, had a sample of some 35,000 households and collected information on household size together with an estimate—albeit very crude—of cash income. The national mean household size was found to be 4.9 persons, taking into account urban areas where households are known to be smaller than in rural areas. Our measurement of the household as a unit, therefore, appears to be compatible with that found in other survey work in Tanzania.

The frequency distribution of households and the population by household size is shown in Table 3.1. Though households with more than ten people are rare (6 per cent), and those with less than three people are more common (19 per cent), a greater percentage of the population lives in large households (16 per cent) than in small households (6 per cent).

The structure of the typical household was nuclear. Heads of household amounted to 18.7 per cent of the population, 54 per cent were their sons or daughters, and 16 per cent were spouses. Only 11 per cent were other relatives of the head and 0.3 per cent were

Table 3.1: Distribution of population and households by household size

Household size	Number of households	Per cent of households	Per cent of population
1	42	7.0	1.3
2	74	12.3	4.7
3	80	13.3	7.5
4	76	12.7	9.6
5	80	13.3	12.6
6	70	11.7	13.2
7	55	9.2	12.0
8	46	7.6	11.6
9	23	3.8	6.5
10	17	2.8	5.3
11–20	38	6.3	15.7
Total	601	100.0	100.0

non-relatives. Furthermore, the population was evenly divided by sex, 50.4 per cent being female and 49.6 per cent male. The age distribution by sex and marital status is given in Table 3.2. For both males and females the proportion of the population in each of the five-year age groups older than the group 15–19 is only around

Table 3.2 Marital status by age group and sex

Age group (years)	No.	Marital status (%)				
		Overall	Single	Married	Divorced	Widowed
Males						
0–4	238	15.2	15.2	—	—	—
5–9	303	19.4	19.4	—	—	—
10–14	276	17.7	17.7	—	—	—
15–19	140	9.0	8.9	0.1	—	—
20–24	74	4.7	3.5	1.3	—	—
25–29	67	4.3	1.0	3.3	0.1	—
30–34	56	3.6	0.3	3.3	—	—
35–39	81	5.2	0.1	4.9	0.2	—
40–44	54	3.5	—	3.2	0.2	0.1
45–49	58	3.7	0.3	3.0	0.4	0.1
50–54	48	3.1	0.1	2.9	0.1	—
55–59	43	2.8	0.2	2.4	0.1	0.1
60 and over	124	7.9	0.4	6.3	0.8	0.4
Total[a]	1 562	100.0	66.9	30.7	1.8	0.6
Females						
0–4	227	14.3	14.3	—	—	—
5–9	274	17.3	17.3	—	—	—
10–14	225	14.2	14.2	—	—	—
15–19	162	10.2	8.1	1.8	0.2	0.1
20–24	108	6.8	2.0	4.2	0.6	0.1
25–29	132	8.3	0.8	6.9	0.6	0.1
30–34	94	5.9	0.2	5.1	0.5	0.1
35–39	88	5.5	0.1	4.5	0.6	0.3
40–44	62	3.9	0.1	3.0	0.4	0.4
45–49	72	4.5	0.1	3.5	0.3	0.6
50–54	48	3.0	—	2.3	0.3	0.4
55–59	22	1.4	0.1	0.8	0.3	0.2
60 and over	73	4.6	—	1.8	0.5	2.3
Total[a]	1 587	100.0	57.1	34.0	4.3	4.6

[a] The sum of the column may not correspond to the total shown owing to rounding.

one-third that of the groups younger than 15–19. This indicates either an increase in the birth rate since 1965, or reduced child mortality, or that there has been substantial out-migration sustained over a long period, with migrants leaving while aged between 15 and 19 years. If migration were the sole explanation then some two-thirds of the age group 15–19 would be leaving the village. We will return to this issue in the next section.

Fifty per cent of women marry between the age of 20–24 and 51 per cent of men marry between the age of 25–29. Of those who had been married, 10 per cent of women and 5 per cent of men are currently divorced. The incidence of divorce does not vary much according to age group.

The educational profile of the population by age and sex is given in Table 3.3. The educational levels of females are significantly lower than those of males. Among those over nine years of age, 50 per cent of females as opposed to 30 per cent of males have no formal schooling. Most people who have had formal schooling have not progressed beyond the lower primary level. Less than 1 per cent of the population has received any secondary education. Even among the age groups 15–24, only 2 per cent have had any secondary education, and 20 per cent have had no schooling at all. Primary education is still not quite universal. Among the age group 10–14, 13 per cent have had no schooling. In Chapter 1, we cited national data which showed that in 1980 some 70 per cent of children in the school age range were currently attending school. Yet we found that in rural areas (which certainly have lower school attendance rates than urban areas) as many as 87 per cent have attended school. The difference is most probably due to the practice, which is fairly wide-spread in Africa, of attending school only intermittently. Thus, some children not currently attending school have attended classes in previous years, and may well rejoin in later years. Thus, the national figures on current attendance give an unduly pessimistic picture of the spread of primary education. The social infrastructure advantages of villagization can be seen both by inference, from this extensive coverage of the child population, and from its probable explanation, the close proximity of households to primary schools. The average distance from home to school was only 0.4 miles, the maximum distance reported being 5 miles.

The other aspect of the education programme noted in Chapter 1 was the Adult Literacy Campaign (ALC). National data show this

Table 3.3: Literacy and education by age and sex

Age group (year)	No.	Level of education (%)					
		Overall	None	Adult lit.	Primary 1–4	Primary 5–8	Secondary
Male							
0–4	238	15.2	15.1	—	0.1	—	—
5–9	303	19.4	15.7	—	3.7	—	—
10–14	276	17.7	2.1	—	12.8	2.7	—
15–19	140	9.0	0.4	0.2	2.4	5.8	0.2
20–24	74	4.7	0.6	0.4	0.8	2.8	0.1
25–29	67	4.3	0.8	0.4	1.1	1.9	—
30–34	56	3.6	0.6	0.4	1.4	1.0	0.1
35–39	81	5.2	1.3	0.8	2.2	0.8	0.1
40–44	54	3.5	0.8	0.8	1.1	0.6	—
45–49	58	3.7	0.8	0.5	1.6	0.8	0.1
50–54	48	3.1	1.1	0.6	0.8	0.4	0.1
55–59	43	2.7	1.1	0.6	0.8	0.2	—
60 and over	124	7.9	4.0	1.8	1.7	0.4	0.1
Total[a]	1 562	100.0	44.6	6.6	30.5	17.6	0.7
Female							
0–4	227	14.3	14.0	—	0.1	0.1	—
5–9	274	17.3	13.6	—	3.6	0.1	—
10–14	225	14.2	1.8	—	9.9	2.5	—
15–19	162	10.2	1.1	0.6	1.4	7.0	0.1
20–24	108	6.8	2.1	0.5	1.2	2.8	0.2
25–29	132	8.3	2.5	1.6	2.5	1.7	0.1
30–34	94	5.9	2.9	1.4	1.4	0.2	—
35–39	88	5.5	2.8	1.2	1.1	0.3	0.1
40–44	62	3.9	2.8	0.9	0.2	—	—
45–49	72	4.5	2.7	1.1	0.4	0.3	—
50–54	48	3.0	1.5	1.3	0.2	—	—
55–59	22	1.4	0.9	0.2	0.1	0.1	—
60 and over	73	4.6	3.1	1.0	0.4	—	—
Total[a]	1 587	100.0	52.0	9.8	22.7	15.1	0.4

[a] The sum of the column may not correspond to the total shown owing to rounding.

to have been successful in reducing adult illiteracy to only 27 per cent by 1977. However, two key issues are whether those who have attended the campaign revert to illiteracy, and whether household heads bother to take part. The latter is important because the head is responsible for many production decisions, and if literacy improves decision-taking, the effect of the campaign on output will be related to the number of household heads it encompassed. Our survey data corroborate the national findings that the Adult Literacy Campaign (ALC) has been highly successful in reaching adults with no formal schooling (see Chapter 1). Overall 36 per cent of males and 31 per cent of females without formal schooling above the age of 14 have attended the classes. Of those attending 61 per cent were female. Furthermore, the classes seem to have been successful in teaching literacy as well as attracting attendance. Sixty-nine per cent of those who have attended, claim that they are now literate. Among household heads, 63 per cent are not literate; in the absence of the ALC only 50 per cent would have been literate. Thus, the ALC has indeed reached decision-takers, but as of 1980 sufficient illiteracy remains to justify a continuation of the campaign.

The macro-data discussed in Chapter 1 raised some doubts about the coverage provided by rural health facilities. In particular, some commentators have suggested that the fact that the number of visits to facilities has not increased, despite an expansion in the number of facilities, indicates a substantial decline in performance. Our survey data on morbidity and utilization of facilities are confined to children under 5 years. One very encouraging finding is that 72 per cent of children under 5 years of age had a health chart issued by the local dispensary or clinic. This shows the extent of contact with health services, which appears to be considerably higher than in a number of more prosperous African economies. The programme of vaccinations also supported this assumption. On average, those children with health charts had been given 3.2 vaccinations. Despite this, the state of health among children appeared to be very poor. It is known from health surveys that about half of all children under 5 years suffer to some degree from protein-energy malnutrition and that for up to 10 per cent of children this condition was very severe. This condition is the single major cause of child mortality. In our survey some 19 per cent of the children with health charts had suffered from severe malnutrition at some stage during their lives. At the time of the survey a large number of the children under 5 years were suffering some form of illness. According to the mothers, during the preceding month 29 per cent were considered to have suffered from malaria, 34 per cent to have had diarrhoea, and 43 per cent to have suffered from a cough or cold. This level of morbidity might seem too high to be credible, but as diarrhoea and colds are both symptoms of malaria the figures corroborate each other, and indeed various other health surveys carried out in Tanzania support the conclusion that the state of health in rural areas is critically poor.

Migration

In Tanzania migration is known to be a phenomenon with a long history which affects a very substantial part of the population. Most studies have focused upon migration from rural to urban areas using data collected in the towns. The pace of urbanization is rapid and, unlike many other African economies, appears to have accelerated in the 1970s relative to the 1960s. Comparison of the 1967 and 1978 Censuses shows that Dar es Salaam grew at around 9 per cent per annum, even granted modest allowances in the figures for boundary changes. Within studies of rural-to-urban migration, attention has been focused upon the roles of rural education and urban wages as inducing migration, and on urban unemployment as retarding migration.[1] Other themes which are recognized as important in other African economies, such as return migration from towns to villages and the size of remittances, have been neglected. It is to these that we now turn.

Some 27 per cent of households have previous members who have migrated out of the village. The concept of 'previous members' is not an easy one, and so it was tightly defined as covering only migrants who were considered to be the (absent) head of the household, spouse of the head, son, or daughter, or a relative currently sending remittances to the household. By this definition, 80 per cent of migrants were sons or daughters of the household head, 15 per cent were other relatives and 5 per cent were either the head or a spouse. The most common reason for migration was 'to seek work'; and those seeking work would head mostly towards Dar es Salaam, whereas those who migrated to other villages went for marriage. Table 3.4 gives a list of destinations according to the reason for migration. Not surprisingly, of the two economic reasons given for migration, those who saw the problem as land shortage moved to other villages and those who saw the problem as work shortage moved to the towns.

In addition to previous members of the household who are now migrants, some current members of the household were previous migrants. These people are of particular interest. Little is known about 'return migrants', since migration surveys have usually been

Table 3.4: Current and returned migrants by reason for migration and destination

| Destination | Current migrants | | | | | Returned migrants (if left since 1970) who had sought work | Probability of return (if seeking work) |
| | Reason for migration | | | | | | |
	To seek work	Marriage	Shortage of land	Other	Total		
Dar es Salaam	44	15	0	13	72 (23.8%)	11	0.20
Other major town	32	7	0	15	54 (17.8%)	14	0.30
Local town	37	7	3	19	66 (21.8%)	32	0.46
Agricultural estate	3	0	2	0	5 (1.6%)	6	0.67
Another village	3	53	18	32	106 (35.0%)	13	0.81
Total	119 (39.3%)	82 (27.1%)	23 (7.6%)	79 (26.1%)	303 (100.0%)	76	0.39

conducted in towns and have missed data on those who have returned.

Altogether, 76 people had left their village to seek work since 1970 and had now returned to live there. Combining this figure with the 119 people who had left to seek work and had not returned gives an overall propensity to return of those who leave to seek work of 39 per cent (76/(76 + 119)). The probability of return according to destination is calculated in the right-hand column of Table 3.4. Although the cell sizes are small, the resulting hierarchy of return propensities is entirely plausible. Most likely to return are those seeking work in another village (81 per cent), next most likely are those seeking work on an agricultural estate (67 per cent); 46 per cent of those going to local towns return, 30 per cent of those going to major towns other than Dar es Salaam, and only 20 per cent of those going to Dar es Salaam itself.

Migrants generally keep in touch with the village. Only a quarter of those who had migrated had never returned to visit the village. When this is combined with the above finding that some 40 per cent of all those who had migrated to seek work were now again resident in the village, it is tempting to infer a circular pattern of migration: job seekers migrate, work away from the village for a few years while retaining their contacts through visits, and finally return to the village to settle. It appears, however, that such an inference would be false, for those currently away from their villages are mostly not at an earlier stage of the same cycle as returned migrants. Rather, migration can be dichotomized into two distinct patterns, short-duration circular migration and permanent one-way migration. Those migrants who had returned to live in the village had mostly been absent from the village for only a short period. Indeed 70 per cent of them had returned either during the year of their departure or in the subsequent year. By contrast, 80 per cent of those currently migrant had already been absent from the village for longer than that.

There are several possible explanations for such a dichotomy. For example, the success or otherwise of the initial job search might be the determining factor: those who were unsuccessful would come back to the village once they had exhausted the means to sustain their search, whereas those who had been successful would stay in employment. Alternatively, the distinct behaviour patterns might reflect different intentions held prior to migration. We investigate the reasons for the different migration patterns by comparing the employment and remittance behaviour of the migrants.

Nearly all migrants had been able to find some means of earning income, so that the difference between the groups is not explained by a failure of return migrants to find any employment. Nor is there a significant difference in the proportion of each group which went into self-employment rather than wage-employment. However, when the levels of earnings and remittances are examined, great differences are revealed (see Table 3.5).

There is no significant difference between the mean earnings of self-employed and wage-earning migrants. Nor is there any difference in the propensity of these two groups to return to the village. However, for both groups there is a big difference between the earnings of migrants who return to the village and of those who stay in the towns.

Returned migrants who had been self-employed had earned only 70 per cent as much as their counterparts who had chosen to stay, whereas returned migrants who had been wage-earners had only 60 per cent of the earnings of their counterparts who had chosen to stay. Of course, part of the explanation for this shortfall is that the reference period for earnings of returned migrants is prior to that of

Table 3.5: Earnings and remittances of current and returned migrants by employment status

	Self-employed		Wage-earners	
	Current	Returned	Current	Returned
N =	25	26	93	87
Mean earnings (shillings/month)	684	485	677	403
% sending money	48	62	55	68
Mean remittance of those sending (sh./month)	94	240	127	223
Total returned (sh./m.)	1 130	3 835	6 470	13 167
% of total earnings remitted	6.6	30.4	10.3	37.6
Mean amount brought back (sh.)	—	419	—	717
% bringing money back	—	81	—	84

current migrants so that wage inflation would produce this type of result. However, over half of the returned migrants had returned to the village as recently as 1979 or 1980 so that wage inflation alone cannot account for such a large difference in earnings, and indeed, since 1974 wage inflation has been modest. The other likely explanation is that those migrants who are the lowest paid are the most likely to come back to the village.

Next we investigate the share of income which is remitted. Among both current and returned migrants, those who were self-employed remitted a significantly lower share of income than those who were wage-earners. We have already noted that there was no significant difference between the mean earnings of the self-employed and wage-earners, so differences in the level of income cannot provide an explanation. However, two differences in job characteristics provide powerful a priori explanations for this result. First, although wage-earners have an even and predictable flow of income over time, the self-employed have a volatile and unpredictable income. Therefore it is more risky to make irretrievable large expenditures such as remittances. Secondly, the self-employed own small businesses for which retained earnings are the primary (and probably the only) source of finance. They, therefore, have both the need and the opportunity for a high investment (savings) rate which would leave little room for non-essential expenditures such as remittances.

For both wage-earners and the self-employed there are major differences between the proportions of income remitted by returned and current migrants. While current migrants were making an average remittance of 10 per cent of income, returned migrants had remitted 35 per cent of income. Moreover, returned migrants were more likely to have made remittances: two-thirds of them, as opposed to half of the numbers of current migrants, had remitted some money.

Combining the data on earnings, remittances, and length of stay yields a picture of two rather distinct migration patterns. Some migrants perhaps do not intend to stay in town for long. While away they accept low-earning jobs rather than spend a long time searching for more highly paid employment. Once in a job they make large remittances and after two years or so return to the village with their accumulated savings. Other migrants, while on the whole they do visit the village, have much looser economic ties. Only half of them make any remittance and the average amount sent by those who do is much smaller. They are unlikely to return to the village to work. One explanation for this might be the system of village land allocation. If a migrant stays away from the village for long he is likely to have his land confiscated by the village council. Hence, migrants must decide swiftly whether to return or to make a life in the towns.

Employment

Labour is the main resource of poor people and of poor economies. Its allocation is therefore of central importance to both the level and the distribution of income. In this section, our main themes of study will be the divisions between farm and non-farm work, between communal and own-account work, and between busy- and slack-season work. However, before embarking on this we need to define the labour force.

A characteristic of many peasant economies is that working members are frequently engaged in more than one economic activity. The survey therefore collected information on both the major and the secondary activities of each household member. This compounds the usual definitional problems surrounding the concept of the labour force, for some respondents had their principal activity outside the labour force, but a secondary activity within it. People who were included in the labour force included that part of the population who were farmers, farm labourers, people engaged in handicrafts, construction and service workers, government employees, members of the armed forces, and other employees. Those of the population who were excluded from the labour force as delimited by the survey were housewives with no farm activities, students, children, the disabled, and those looking for work. In the conventional definition of the labour force, those looking for work would be included, but in the context of rural Africa it was considered clearer to exclude this category. However, as the number of people in this category was negligible, a different classification would have made virtually no difference. Having decided which activities determined the labour force, respondents aged over twelve whose major or secondary activity fell within this list were included in the labour force. The age limitation was arbitrarily chosen.

A majority of the population was not included in the labour force thus defined, the dependency ratio (the ratio of the population not in the labour force to the labour force) being 1.36. It was found that

Table 3.6: Dependency by household size

Household size	Population		Labour force		Dependency ratio
	No.	%	No.	%	
1–2	190	6.0	170	12.6	0.12
3	240	7.5	159	11.8	0.51
4	304	9.5	156	11.6	0.95
5	400	12.6	174	12.9	1.30
6	426	13.4	164	12.2	1.60
7	378	11.9	143	10.6	1.65
8–9	368	11.6	113	8.4	2.26
10	376	11.8	128	9.5	1.94
11+	502	15.8	142	10.5	2.53
Total	3 184	100.0	1 349	100.0	1.36

the dependency ratio differs radically according to household size (see Table 3.6), ranging from 0.12 in one- and two-person households to over 2.5 in the largest households. This is the first indication of a topic to which we will return in detail, namely, that if the data are not carefully adjusted to take household economies of scale into account, differences in household size are likely to dominate all other factors in measured income inequality.

Table 3.7 represents the matrix of main occupation by secondary occupation. It shows that 1,361 people were classified as actively employed by virtue of their main occupation, and of these 316 were also actively employed in a secondary occupation. A further 54 people were actively employed in secondary occupations only, but were still included in the labour force. Almost all those who were not actively employed were either students or the disabled. As many as 90 per cent of the labour force gave their main or only occupation as farming, while the remaining 10 per cent were evenly spread among the other occupations. There is, then, a strong preponderance of farmers in the village labour force. Fewer farmers than non-farmers engage in multiple activities: only 20 per cent of farmers said they had a secondary occupation whereas 60 per cent of non-farmers had a secondary occupation (which was only in 11 per cent of cases farming).

The survey also collected data on the number of days spent working on each activity over two reference periods—the year and the

Table 3.7: Main occupation by secondary occupation for those aged over 12

Main occupation	Second occupation							
	Actively employed (AE)							
	Farmer	Farm labourer	Handicraft	Construction	Service	Government	Other	Sub-total (AE)
Farmer	—	4	66	43	30	7	121	271
Farm labourer	8				1			9
Handicraft	5							5
Construction	2							2
Service	13				2		1	16
Government	7				4		1	11
Other								1
Regular army								
National service							1	1
Sub-total (AE)	35	4	66	43	37	7	124	316
Housewife								
Disabled	1		1					2
Student	9		1		25		16	51
Looking for job	1							1
Sub-total (NAE)	11		2		25		16	54
Total (AE) + (NAE)	46	4	68	43	62	7	140	370

Main occupation	Second occupation					
	Not actively employed (NAE)					
	None	Housewife	Student	Looking for job	Sub-total (NAE)	Total (AE) + (NAE)
Farmer	464	545	0	4	1 013	1 284
Farm labourer	2				2	2
Handicraft	3	3			6	15
Construction						5
Service	3	3		1	7	9
Government	7	3			10	26
Other	4	3			7	18
Regular army						1
National service						1
Sub-total (AE)	484	557	0	5	1 045	1 361
Housewife	12				12	12
Disabled	49	1			50	52
Student	331	9			320	371
Looking for job	2				2	3
Sub-total (NAE)	374	10	0	0	384	438
Total (AE) + (NAE)	858	567	0	5	1 429	1 799

busy season. On average, members of the labour force worked 226 days each year. Combined with information from Table 3.7, this suggests that there was little labour surplus in the village. Only three people could be described as unemployed (principal activity 'looking for job') and, excluding students, the total population not actively employed aged over 12, including the disabled, was only 64. However, even if all of these were set to work, the labour force would increase by less than 5 per cent.

Labour allocation over the year by occupation and activity is shown in Table 3.8. Three sets of activities account for 98 per cent of total labour input. Work on own holding absorbs 65 per cent of labour, work on the communal farm absorbs 24 per cent, and work on non-farm activities within the village absorbs a further 9 per cent. Work on other farms and work outside the village are both negligible. Combining this with the data on migration and occupation we may infer that most households do not participate in any labour market. Few households have employment-related migration experience, and the number of household members who work either in the farm labour market within the village or in any labour market outside the village is negligible. Finally, few farmers have non-farm secondary occupations within the village, since much of the non-farm work is being done by non-farmers with multiple non-farm occupations. Conversely, non-farmers do disproportionately little communal farm work—only 14 per cent of their work time—whereas farmers spend as much as 24 per cent of all days worked on communal farm work.

Table 3.8 also gives mean earnings per day worked for those with positive earnings. Communal farm work was effectively unremunerated (this is discussed below). Farm work either in or out of the village was paid at rates in the range of 10–16 shillings per day, while non-farm work was paid in the range of 30–60 shillings per day. We return to earnings in more detail when we consider income.

The second frame of reference for work was the busy season. Those in the labour force were asked to specifiy the period of the year which they regarded as busy. The answers suggested that although within villages there is a busy season, how well defined it is and when it occurs varies among villages according to their ecology and geographical location. In some villages everyone identifies particular months as busy and others as slack. In other villages there is much less consensus about busy and slack seasons, indicating a

Table 3.8: *Labour allocation and earnings by main occupation and activity*

Occupation	Activity						Total
	Own farm	Communal farm	Other farms in village	Other farms outside village	Off-farm in village	Off-farm outside village	
Not specified	0.2	0	—	—	0	—	0.3
Housewife	1.1	0.4 (0.6)[a]	0 (15)	—	0.1	0	1.6
Farmer	62.4	22.8 (3.8)	0.6 (10.1)	0.3 (13.9)	7.0 (34.4)	0.8 (43.9)	93.6
Farm labourer	–	–	0.1 (10)	0 (16)	–	–	0.1
Handicrafts	0.3	0	—	—	0.3 (35)	0.1 (63.4)	0.7
Construction	0.1	0 (3.3)	—	—	0.2 (41.2)	—	0.3
Service	0.1	0.1	—	—	0.3 (27)	—	0.5
Government	0.3	0.1	0.1 (14)	—	0.5 (47)	0.2 (34.1)	1.1
Other	0.2	0.1	—	—	0.6 (31.9)	0 (58.8)	1.0
Disabled	0.1	0.1	—	—	0	—	0.1
Army	–	–	—	—	0	—	0
National service	–	0	—	—	0	—	0
Student	0.2	–	—	—	–	—	0.2
Looking for work	–	–	—	—	–	—	—
Total	65	23.6	0.8	0.3	9	1.1	100

[a] In each cell the upper figure is the percentage of labour allocation and the lower figure in parentheses the mean earnings in shillings per day worked, for those receiving positive earnings. 0 signifies less than 0.1 per cent and — stands for zero.

more even pattern of labour input over the year. Table 3.9 shows the pattern of seasonal peaks by village. The entries show the percentage of all households in a village which picked out month 'x' as being part of the busy season for the household. The figures in bold type are all observations over 90 per cent. For villages where no single month was cited by over 90 per cent of households, the next highest months are given in italics. In every village there is a single peak period of months so identified, and such consensus reinforces the impression of the reliability of individual responses.

The busy season is defined with reference to work on own holdings. Therefore, by definition more labour is provided on own holdings in a typical month of the busy season than in a typical month of the year as a whole. We now investigate whether this seasonal pattern of labour input on the owner-operated holding is offset by a counter-seasonal pattern of labour input into all other activities. In Table 3.10 we present the total number of days worked per month, excluding days worked on own holdings, for the busy season normalized against the year as a whole. For example, the top left-hand entry, 1.04, indicates that farmers worked 4 per cent more days per month on the communal shamba during the busy season than during the year as a whole. In fact, the data show that during the busy season 30 per cent more days are worked off-shamba than during the year as a whole. Thus, instead of being counter-cyclical, shamba and off-shamba work are synchronized. Breaking down by activity, we find that work on the communal shamba is evenly spread throughout the year. This is consistent with the common practice of setting work norms of one or two days per week which run through the year. Excluding both own-shamba and communal shamba work, remaining employment appears to be heavily pro-cyclical: during the busy season, non-shamba employment is 90 per cent above the average for the year. One possible explanation for this observation might be that non-shamba work produces inputs for, or uses inputs from, shamba work so that the two have to be synchronized. An alternative explanation is that because most income is generated during the busy season, it is the time when demand is at its peak. The slack season would then be a period of Keynesian demand-constrained supply which might manifest itself as fewer days worked.

This might appear to contradict our previous suggestion that there is little surplus labour. However, it should be remembered that

Table 3.9: Busy season by village^a

Village	Jan.	Feb.	Mar.	Apr.	May	June	July	Aug.	Sep.	Oct.	Nov.	Dec.
1	**99**	**99**	**97**	**97**	88	85	63	7	22	**94**	**100**	**99**
2	71	74	**97**	**97**	**93**	88	84	80	88	88	88	88
3	82	**91**	**91**	**91**	**93**	45	13	4	7	7	7	11
4	**99**	**100**	**100**	**92**	88	77	50	12	0	0	0	12
5	**97**	**96**	**97**	**90**	84	61	47	34	25	22	22	25
6	**100**	**100**	**100**	**100**	**93**	89	0	6	**100**	**100**	**100**	**100**
7	**100**	**100**	**100**	**100**	77	77	2	2	2	78	87	**100**
8	**100**	**100**	**100**	**100**	28	20	5	0	0	34	**97**	**100**
9	**100**	**100**	**100**	**100**	**100**	**100**	48	14	5	5	25	**100**
10	**92**	**91**	**95**	**95**	**95**	**95**	77	29	0	51	83	**92**
11	21	37	*92*	*85*	*85*	*81*	*79*	*75*	*75*	*70*	16	6
12	*71*	*77*	47	41	24	23	21	11	36	*56*	*55*	*53*
13	*81*	25	20	20	11	11	11	3	0	0	66	**100**
14	0	0	7	67	**100**	**100**	**100**	**100**	**100**	**100**	36	0
15	7	7	15	**99**	**100**	**100**	**100**	**100**	**100**	**90**	43	7
16	**98**	**100**	**100**	**100**	16	17	17	17	**100**	**98**	**98**	**98**
17	**94**	**96**	**96**	72	11	8	4	4	2	2	49	49
18	68	70	64	75	75	59	50	52	77	*84*	*84*	*87*
19	**100**	**100**	**100**	**100**	**100**	6	3	3	3	**99**	**99**	**99**
20	**98**	**93**	**93**	0	0	0	2	2	2	2	0	**98**

The figures in bold type are all observations over 90 per cent. For villages where no single month was cited by over 90 per cent of households, the next highest months are given in italics.

Table 3.10: The seasonality of non-shamba activities

Days worked per month during the busy season normalized on days worked per month through the year by activity

Occupational group	Communal shamba	All occupations other than own shamba and communal shamba	All occupations other than own shamba
Farmers	1.04	1.81	1.25
Non-farmers	0.58	2.22	1.84
All	1.02	1.90	1.30

over the year as a whole, virtually 90 per cent of days worked are accounted for by the own-shamba and the communal shamba. Hence, even the pronounced seasonality of non-shamba work does not represent a dramatic level of surplus labour in the slack season. If the labour days per month on non-shamba work were maintained through the year at the rate observed during the busy season, and this caused no reduction in other work activities, then the annual total labour input would rise by 10 per cent.

The importance of communal activities to farmers during the busy season is revealed when the labour input off-own-shamba is broken down by occupation and activity. Some 54 per cent of this labour input is spent on the communal shamba, with a further 14 per cent spent on communal non-shamba work. Therefore, during the busy season, communal activities account for 68 per cent of the work done off-own-shamba. For farmers the percentage is even higher at 76 per cent. Work on own business, 80 per cent of which is done by farmers, accounts for 13 per cent of total work, while all forms of wage employment, about 50 per cent of which is done by farmers, account for nearly 20 per cent of work. Details are shown in Table 3.11.

As mentioned earlier, those whose main occupation is non-farm make up 10 per cent of the labour force. From Table 3.9 we find that this group provides only 3 per cent of the labour input to the communal shamba during the year as a whole. From Tables 3.10 and 3.11 we find that during the busy season, non-farmers provide an even smaller share of communal farm work. Nor is this offset by communal non-shamba work, for the group provides only 8 per cent of the labour input into these activities.

Table 3.11: Busy season labour allocation off own shamba by selected activities and occupations (per cent)

Main occupation	Activity				
	Work for wages	Communal shamba	Communal non-shamba	Own business	All
Housewife	—	0.8	0.1	0.2	1.1
		0.9[a]	0.1	0.1	
Farmer	10.7	52.2	12.8	10.2	85.9
	5.0	54.0	24.5	7.6	
Farm labourer	0.2	—	—	—	0.2
	0.1				
Handicraft	0.8	0.2	0.1	1.0	2.1
	0.3	0.3	0.1	0.5	
Construction	0.5	0.1	—	0.2	0.8
	0.2	0.1	0.1	0.1	
Service	0.9	0.2	0.6	0.3	1.9
	0.4	0.1	0.1	0.2	
Government	3.1	0.1	0.2	—	3.5
	1.2	0.4	0.3	0.1	
Other	2.6	0.3	0.2	0.3	3.4
	1.0	0.4	0.1	0.1	
Disabled	—	—	—	0.1	0.1
		0.1		0.1	
Regular army	0.3	—	—	0.1	0.4
	0.1			0.1	
National service	0.3	—	—	0.3	0.5
	0.1			0.1	
Total	19.4	53.9	13.9	12.7	100.0

[a] In each cell the upper figure is the percentage of labour allocation and the lower figure is the percentage of labour force involved.

To conclude, labour allocation is dominated by own-shamba work and communal activities, primarily the communal shamba. Over the year as a whole own-shamba work accounts for 65 per cent of total labour input and communal work about 30 per cent, of which 24 per cent is on the communal shamba. Farmers appear to do a disproportionate amount of communal work of all types compared to non-farmers. Surplus labour does not appear to be extensive, for virtually everyone who can work does work. If everyone in the labour force worked five days per week for 50 weeks per year instead of for the length of time they do now, total labour input would rise by a third. But this is clearly well beyond the feasible maximum labour input. It seems likely that an increase in the demand for labour beyond 10–20 per cent would be met only by displacing existing activities and that a substantial proportion of *any* increase in labour demand would be met by displacing existing activities.

Assets

Other than their own labour, Tanzanian peasant households have only a limited range of assets. Financial assets are negligible (yielding a heavily negative real return), and machinery and equipment are confined to the most rudimentary of items, as are household goods. Undoubtedly the major assets are land and livestock.

The creation of villages provided the government with an opportunity to redistribute land and we are able to assess the extent of this land reform. However, in most of Tanzania land is abundant and so we would expect its distribution to be determined predominantly by the availability of household labour. The distribution of landholdings shown in Table 3.12 largely confirms this presumption. The degree of inequality in the distribution of land between households appears to be lower than in other African countries. The Gini coefficient of land concentration was 0.35 compared to 0.42 in Mozambique (traditional sector), 0.55 in Kenya (registered small-

Table 3.12: Size distribution of landholdings, 1980

Size (acres)	Households (per cent)	Land area (per cent)	Average size (acres)	Mean household size	Per capita holding (acres)
0–1	6.6	1.1	0.8	3.5	0.23
1–2	12.3	4.6	1.8	3.5	0.51
2–3	20.5	11.8	2.7	4.4	0.61
3–4	15.0	11.8	3.7	5.1	0.73
4–6	22.5	24.5	5.2	5.6	0.93
6–8	10.9	16.4	7.1	6.7	1.05
8–12	9.4	19.8	10.0	7.6	1.32
12+	2.8	10.0	16.7	9.9	1.70
Total	100.0	100.0	4.7	5.4	0.87

holdings), 0.55 in Somalia, and 0.64 in Ghana.[2] Further, most of this
concentration is accounted for by differences in household size.
Another indication of the lack of pressure upon land is that the
incidence of landlessness is negligible, only 1 per cent of households
reporting on land no holding. Unlike the situation in rural Asia, landlessness is not a significant variable in explaining poverty.

We have suggested that the relative equity of land distribution is
due to the fact that land is abundant. However, in 1974 the Tanzanian Government relocated the majority of the rural population in
newly created villages through Operation Sogeza, and this opportunity for land reform might itself account for the lack of land concentration. The extent of such land redistribution is investigated in
Table 3.13 which presents a matrix of landholdings at present by
those prior to villagization. Overall, the degree of land concentration
was virtually unaltered by villagization, indeed concentration even
slightly increased, the bottom 40 per cent of holders having 19 per
cent of the land area prior to Sogeza and 18 per cent currently.
Considering that communal farms are jointly owned, land ownership as a whole may be more equal than the private component
alone would suggest. It may be that everybody has less private land
since villagization precisely because part of the land is now communal. This is not to suggest that Sogeza exacerbated inequalities,
but it should be remembered that the primary objective was to
create villages and concentrate scattered households so that they
might benefit from government services. That it was not a land
reform can be seen by the very limited extent to which households
moved between size classes. For example, from Table 3.13 we find
that 58 per cent of those households who held less than 1 acre and 70
per cent of those households who held more than 12 acres prior to
Sogeza still do so. Overall, 60 per cent of households remained in the
same size class and a further 20 per cent changed only to the neigh-
bouring size class. Not all the changes recorded in Table 3.13 are
due to reallocation of land by the Village Council. Land can be
acquired through inheritance or illegally bought and sold. Those
changes which have occurred because of reallocation by a Village
Council appear to be slightly equalizing. Those households with
larger holdings also received the largest allocations, though these
were generally not proportionately as large as the share of land they
held from other sources. Thus, 43 per cent of the land area held by
households with less than 1 acre was acquired through the Village

Table 3.13: Land redistribution since villagization

Distribution of landholdings now (acres)	Distribution of landholdings before villagization (acres) (%)								
	0–1	1–2	2–3	3–4	4–5	6–8	8–12	12+	Total
0–1	3 (58)	1 (6)	0 (1)	—	1 (3)	0 (2)	—	—	5
1–2	1 (21)	6 (53)	2 (9)	1 (7)	0 (2)	0 (3)	—	—	11
2–3	1 (17)	2 (14)	12 (67)	3 (17)	3 (13)	0 (3)	—	—	20
3–4	—	2 (14)	2 (9)	7 (47)	3 (11)	2 (13)	0 (3)	—	15
4–6	0 (4)	1 (10)	2 (10)	3 (21)	15 (63)	1 (10)	1 (11)	0 (5)	24
6–8	—	0 (2)	1 (4)	1 (7)	1 (5)	8 (59)	0 (5)	—	11
8–12	—	0 (2)	—	0 (1)	0 (4)	1 (10)	6 (78)	1 (25)	10
12+	—	—	—	—	0 (1)	—	0 (3)	3 (70)	4
Total	5 (100)	11 (100)	17 (100)	16 (100)	25 (100)	13 (100)	8 (100)	4 (100)	100

[a] In each cell the upper figure is the percentage of the total number of households and the lower figure in parentheses is the percentage of the column total. 0 signifies less than 0.5 per cent and — stands for zero.

Council (0.36 acres per holding), compared with only 22 per cent of the land area of those with over 12 acres (3.64 acres per holding).

More striking than the stability of land concentration in the changes made by Operation Sogeza, is the change in the mean size of holdings. From Table 3.12 the current mean size of a holding was found to be only 4.7 acres, whereas prior to Operation Sogeza it had been 5.2 acres. This 10 per cent reduction in holding size is sufficiently large to require explanation. Since the sample of households is the same in each case, the finding cannot be ascribed to sampling error. Further, any biases in estimating land area would be common to both figures. We must therefore look beyond explanations in terms of measurement error. One possibility is that the creation of villages has directly reduced holding size by creating land scarcity. Instead of a scattered population resident on holdings, the population is now resident in the village and travels to the holdings. In turn, this makes land holdings which are close to the villages more valuable than those further away and defines a margin of distance beyond which it is not economic to cultivate, either because too much time is wasted walking to the holding, or because the transportation of inputs and outputs is too arduous.

A second possibility stems from the profile of labour allocation described in the previous section. The creation of villages has enabled the development of a range of communal activities which draw upon household labour. In Tables 3.8 and 3.11 it was indicated that communal activities take up a considerable proportion of labour time. If we are correct in regarding labour availability as the principal (though by no means only) determinant of landholding, then a reduction in labour time available for the cultivation of the private holding would indeed reduce chosen holding size. Unfortunately, we have not been able to choose between these two possible explanations, though it is agreed that both would apply to some degree.

A priori, land abundance seems an unlikely characteristic of an economy in which the mean holding size is less than 5 acres. However, the small holding size is determined by the predominant hand-hoe technology. Given this technology, there are few economies of scale to be gained from amalgamating plots but there is something to be gained by way of spreading risks and controlling disease if holdings are made up of spatially distinct plots. The average household holds its 4.7 acreas in 2.5 plots. In some developing countries inheritance laws combine with impediments to land trans-actions to create excessive land fragmentation, but no such problem has arisen in Tanzania. Only 6 per cent of households had more than four plots, the greatest number of plots found in the survey being seven.

We started our discussion of assets by suggesting that only two assets were important in the context of Tanzanian peasant agricul-ture, namely, land and livestock. Our discussion of land allocation has suggested that it is not a very powerful differentiating asset owing to its abundance. Moreover, it is largely an unmarketable asset since its purchase or sale is illegal. Livestock, on the other hand, is both scarce and fully marketable. Nationally, Tanzania has an enormous stock of cattle but much of this belongs to nomadic pastoralists. Among the settled farm population, ownership of live-stock is relatively rare as is shown in Table 3.14. Chickens are the only form of livestock found in most households. Sheep and goats are the next most common, being found in 30 per cent of households; whereas high-value livestock—improved cattle (cattle bred partly from imported stock)—are owned by only a little over 2 per cent of households. In a sense, 'livestocklessness' is the Tanzanian counter-part to landlessness in rural Asia, that is, it is the best indicator of an absence of marketable assets, and it is this which differentiates the rural population into two sizeable groups. Table 3.14 suggests further that among those who own livestock it is likely to be a

Table 3.14: Ownership of livestock

Livestock	Per cent of all households	Mean number of livestock owned by those with some stock
Improved bulls	2	9
Improved cows	2	2
Unimproved bulls	17	3
Unimproved cows	23	9
Oxen	3	4
Sheep and goats	30	11
Pigs	3	6
Chickens	64	13
Ducks and geese	5	9

substantial source of income. Only around 20 per cent of households own any cattle, but among these households, the mean number held is approximately 12. Although this does not represent a large herd it may generate a significant income in an economy where the average size of holding is below 5 acres. When we turn to our analysis of income differentiation, we find that livestock ownership is indeed a decisive factor in explaining income inequality.

Income

The typical peasant household is a highly complex business conglomerate engaged in a wide range of distinct economic activities and facing decisions on resource allocation in the presence of enormous risk and uncertainty. Typically this business will generate a pitifully small income. This combination of complexity and smallness makes the analysis of peasant income peculiarly difficult at both the practical and the conceptual levels. The practical problems relate to gathering data on a large and disparate range of tiny income sources. The conceptual problems relate to a measure of income which can approximate to a credible indicator of the welfare of the household. Although models which derive and hence predict the optimal behaviour of industrial firms are commonplace in economics, optimizing models of peasant households are still too rudimentary to be usable except when the environment is unusually simple.

We now built up household income from four components: *crop output*, *livestock income*, *non-farm income*, and *remittances received*. Of these crop income requires the most complex treatment. The reference period for all income sources is the twelve months preceding the survey.

Crop output

Over 98 per cent of village households surveyed had grown some crops in the preceding year. The survey asked about 23 identified crops, 21 of which were indeed grown by the surveyed farmers. In addition, some crops not specified in the survey were grown and are included under the category 'other crops'. The average farmer grew three different crops. The decision to grow several crops rather than to specialize may be based on utilizing endowments of land and

labour to maximize income. Alternatively, the decision may be more
complex. For example, it may matter whether the crop is a food crop
or not, and how closely related the yield risks of different crops are.
In fact, the most common crops were food crops. Maize was grown
by 89 per cent of households, the other common crops being
sorghum (34 per cent), beans (34 per cent), and cassava (27 per
cent)—all these being basic food crops. The only widespread non-
food crop grown entirely for cash was coffee, which was grown by 20
per cent of the surveyed farmers. Table 3.15 shows by crop the
percentage of farmers growing the crop, the mean acreage of those
growing the crop, the mean yield per acre, and the mean price
received per kilo when the crop was sold. Acreage is adjusted for
multiple cropping: a double-cropped acreage is converted into two
single-cropped areas of half the size.

The figures reported in Table 3.15 are broadly in line with previous estimates of yield and price. By far the most important crop is
maize, and for this crop the yield, at 313 kilos per acre, is some
10–20 per cent lower than the national estimates of the Marketing
Development Bureau. These national estimates, however, are by no
means firmly based and do not constitute grounds for upward re-
vision of the yields found in the survey. There are more grounds for
doubting the survey figure for the price at which maize was sold, 1.2
shillings per kilo. Although the official price for maize purchases was
only 1 shilling per kilo, coexisting with the official market is an
unofficial market in which prices are considerably higher, though
subject to much spatial and temporal variation. It is possible that
households were reluctant to divulge accurate information on unofficial marketings (although such transactions are not illegal), and so
our survey may understate cash income from the sale of food crops.
Since most unofficial marketings are purely local transactions, being
in the form of sales among peasant households, such an under-
estimate does not affect the amount of cash that households have
available to buy urban goods. We will return to the issue of the
pricing of food crops when we consider the valuation of subsistence
food consumption. First, however, we will discuss income from
marketed crop output.

Whether crop growing generates a net income for a household in
addition to the output which it directly consumes, depends upon
whether gross sales of crops exceed the costs of producing crops. We
will define the value of own consumption as being the value of all

Table 3.15: *The cropping pattern*

Crop	Percentage of households growing crop	Mean acreage[a]	Mean yield (kg./acre)	Mean price (sh./kg.)	Gross mean/ yield per acre (sh.)
Maize	89	1.74	313	1.20	376
Sorghum	34	1.57	213	1.17	249
Beans	34	0.88	209	3.46	723
Cassava	27	1.06	244	0.77	188
Bananas	20	1.16	3 229	0.77	2 486
Coffee	20	1.28	193	5.67	1 094
Ground nuts	19	1.24	82	14.03	1 150
Millet	18	2.40	178	1.31	233
Rice	7	1.14	154	3.54	545
Sweet potatoes	5	0.75	404	1.92	776
Cashew	3	1.97	165	1.60	264
Coconuts	3	3.27	122	1.50	183
Yams	3	0.65	637	2.31	1 471
Sesame	2	0.82	134	6.62	887
Sunflower	2	1.00	234	1.92	449
Tobacco	2	0.77	49	3.77	185
Peas	1	0.85	232	3.25	754
Sugar cane	1	0.96	2 137	1.00	2 137
Wheat	0	2.00	—	—	—
Cotton	0	1.00	600	1.00	600
Tea	0	1.00	—	—	—
Others	15	0.80	412	2.38	981

[a] Of those households growing the crop.

food produced and consumed within the household. This is, of course, a concept of gross output since no production costs are deducted. We further define the costs of crop production as including all cash expenditures on wages and inputs and also the value of own produced inputs, but excluding the value of household labour used in producing the crops. Mean production costs defined in this way were not high, being 216 shillings per household, of which 99 shillings were for purchased inputs and 117 shillings represented the value of own-produced inputs. However, with the above definition of own consumption, all these production costs must be netted out from crop sales. Thus a household which made no crop sales but had the mean production costs would have an own consumption of 216 shillings in excess of crop income. Net crop income excluding own consumption, would therefore be 216 shillings. Analogously, a household which had gross crop sales of 216 shillings would have a net crop income less own consumption of zero. We term this income component 'net crop sales', but it must be understood in the context of subsistence consumption income. A negative income from 'net crop sales' does not mean that a household is losing money by selling crops, but rather that it is not making enough to cover total crop production costs, so that own consumption exceeds crop income. The household needs to generate non-crop income in order to finance its own level of consumption of crops.

All households growing crops had some production costs and so all had non-zero net income from crop sales, although for a few households this was negative. The mean gross value of crop sales was 779 shillings per annum and so net income from crop sales averaged 558 shillings.

We now consider the valuation of subsistence consumption. To be converted into income, the quantity of food which is grown and then consumed by the household must be valued. This poses a conceptual problem, for there are several procedures which might be used to assign prices and no single procedure is unquestionably correct. Here we present three possibilities: first, consider the case in which a household sells part of a particular crop and consumes the rest. In such a situation, we are able to gather information on the price which the household received per kilo for that part of the crop which it sold. This price could then be used to value the part of the crop which was consumed. There are two problems with this approach. One is that it would leave much own consumption still to be valued

by some different procedure. As an illustration of the second problem, consider two households which consume the same quantities of
maize but sell maize at different prices. Even if the household which
achieved the higher price could have sold all its maize at the higher
price, it would presumably have had to buy maize at a higher price.
We may presume this since otherwise the household would have
sold its own maize and bought other maize, and if it had done this
we would not observe own consumption. Therefore different selling
prices must also reflect different buying prices. But differences in
buying prices, while they constitute a standard index number problem, do not constitute differences in income. That is, two households
buying 1 kilo of maize each but at different prices have a common
value of maize consumption somewhere between the maize expenditure of each household. Hence, it would overstate differences in
income to value own consumption at the market prices achieved by
individual households.

   The second method which may be adopted is to calculate the
mean price achieved for all the sales of each crop. For example, the
mean price of maize sold by farmers was 1.2 shillings and this price
can be used to value all own consumption. This is the procedure
most commonly used in budget surveys. On this procedure the mean
value of own consumption for the 583 crop-growing households was
1,641 shillings per annum. The problem with this approach is that,
although it provides a sensible estimate of mean income, it can
exaggerate differences in income between households. Households
which grow and eat high-priced crops generally have a much higher
income than households which eat low-priced crops. The issue is
analogous to our previous case of two households facing different
maize prices. If the household which eats high-priced food could sell
the food it currently eats when it wanted to at average market prices,
and be certain of buying low-priced food whenever it wanted to at
average market prices, then indeed, the household which consumes
high-priced foods has a higher income. By contrast, if the household
cannot rely on being able to buy or grow the low-priced foods, then
its consumption of high-priced foods merely reflects the fact that it is
forced to pay a higher unit price for a given quantity of 'food'. In this
case, we are back at the index number problem that 'food' is consumed at two different prices and needs to be valued at some average. Additionally, there is the problem of aggregating crops into
'food' without using market prices.

The third method, which we consider the most reliable is to measure the food content of a crop by its calorie equivalent. Own consumed crops are converted into the calories they contain so that for each household we have a measurement of total own consumption in units of calories. Using the procedure described in the second method above, we then calculate the value of all food consumed, at mean market prices. Dividing the total value of the own food consumption of the sample by the calorie content of this food yields a mean price per calorie. The value of own food consumption for a particular household is then the quantity of calories contained in the food it consumes multiplied by this mean price per calorie. This approach has two advantages. First, it eliminates exaggerated income differences between households resulting from whether the crop they need to grow in order to survive would have a high or low market price it if were sold. If in fact there are some households which, having a high income for other reasons, therefore choose to consume a high-value crop rather than sell it, it is true that our procedure will understate income inequality. However, the high-income households will still be identified as having a high income (though less than its true value) so they will not be misidentified. By contrast, if only the second procedure is used, some households which have no choice but to grow and consume high-priced crops will appear to be high-income even if all other income sources and calorie consumption are below average. Thus, the second procedure leads to a serious misidentification of the poor (serious because own consumption is a large component of income). Misidentification of poor and non-poor households is a critical pitfall because. it obstructs the proper analysis of poverty: the apparent poor manifest different characteristics from the true poor.

The second advantage is that while differences between households are reflected more accurately by using the third procedure, the estimate of the mean value per household of own consumption is the same whether that procedure or the second is used. Therefore, mean total income and the mean composition of income are unaffected by the adoption of our proposal. This enables us to compare the results with other surveys which have used the second procedure.

As well as identifying the poor more accurately, the change to calorie valuation reduces the overall inequality of income. The coefficient of variation falls from 118.9 to 105.8 which is the lowest value for any income component in the survey. We would indeed expect subsistence food consumption to be more equally distributed than other income components if only because the income elasticity of demand for food is invariably less than unity.

Fundamentally, the choice of procedure for the valuation of subsistence consumption depends upon the characteristics of the marketing system in which peasants operate. This is why different procedures are appropriate in different economies. For economies in which peasants face reliable, well-integrated markets with low transaction costs our chosen procedure would be quite inappropriate. However, Tanzanian rural market networks are far removed from such a characterization. All non-food crops are marketed through monopoly bureaucracies with very high transaction costs and poor records both for crop collection and for making payments. All inter-district maize transactions (over 30 kilos)[3] are similarly the monopoly of the National Milling Corporation. This agency has been overwhelmed by the transport and storage problems involved in collecting maize for urban consumption. It was never designed as a mechanism for delivering maize for *rural* consumption and has neither the information system nor the satisfactory transportation facilities to perform such a role. The effect of its legal monopoly has therefore been to close down much of the intra-rural maize market, leaving only a small illegal inter-district trade which suffers high transaction costs precisely because of its illegality. Therefore, peasants cannot rely upon crop markets to make food purchases as and when they require food. Instead, they must rely primarily upon storing their own food production.[4]

However, the grain storage facilities of most households in Tanzania are very poor, and it is not generally possible for a household to store grain for much longer than twelve months. (Indeed with soft grains such as *katamani* maize storage periods are considerably shorter). Hence, food consumption is restricted to current subsistence production plus a limited quantity of market purchases.

Because the survey did not gather information on the consumption of purchased food we are able to estimate only the calorie intake due to subsistence consumption. The calorie value per kilo of particular crops, shown in Table 3.16, can be used both for evaluating subsistence production, as discussed above, and to estimate the calorie intake from that source. Subsistence crop calorie intake per capita was found to be around 1,500 calories per day. First, we compare this with the level of consumption of official supplies of

Table 3.16: Calorie content of East African food crops

Food	Calories per kilo
Maize	3 630
Sorghum	3 350
Beans	1 040
Cassava	1 530
Bananas	1 280
Groundnuts	3 320
Millet	3 360
Rice	3 540
Sweet potato	1 140
Cashew	5 900
Coconut	3 750
Peas	3 370
Yam	1 040
Sugar cane	600
Wheat	3 440
Others	1 000 (assumed)

Source: M. C. Latham, *Human Nutrition in Tropical Africa* (Rome, FAO, 1965), Appendix 3.

maize and rice which was achieved by the population of Dar es Salaam during the same period. In 1979–80 Dar es Salaam received 53 per cent of all National Milling Corporation supplies of maize (108,300 tons), and 61 per cent of all rice supplied (32,600 tons). The population can be estimated quite reliably since there was a Census in 1978, indicating it to be around 840,000. Converting the amount of food into calorie yields gives an estimate of 1,500 calories per capita per day, which is the same as the level of peasant reliance upon subsistence consumption. The analogy between peasant subsistence crop consumption and the purchases of official crop supplies by the urban population is appropriate because both are sources of supply which are sheltered from market prices, and may also provide a more reliable source of supply than the sporadic amounts available on the limited open market. Except in years of most severe drought, the peasant will always have subsistence output, while the population of Dar es Salaam is similarly protected by the supply of food through imports and/or foreign aid. Between 1974 and 1982, official maize and rice supplies to Dar es Salaam fluctuated only in the range 1,100–1,700 calories per capita despite enormous changes in open market availability. Therefore, both the peasantry and the urban population rely to the same extent upon the open market for necessary food purchases. Since the average person consumes around 2,000 vegetable calories per day (an adult male requires around 2,500 calories, see Table 4.1), this suggests that in both urban and rural areas around a quarter of food crop supplies are met by open market purchases.

In addition to calorie and income data, Table 3.15 provides information on land use. Grouping crops into food crops and cash crops reveals that while 68 per cent of land area is devoted to food crops, only 7.6 per cent of land area is used for cash crops, the remaining 24 per cent of land area being left fallow or used for crops which cannot readily be categorized. Thus the ratio of food land to cash crop land is 9 : 1. This has important implications for the estimation of trends in national food supplies. Estimates of these trends differ widely, but the main factor which is commonly cited in support of the higher estimates has been a hypothesized switch out of cash crops. The above evidence in land use, however, makes it apparent that any such change has only a marginal effect upon food output. To demonstrate this, we first take account of the fact that the major cash crops are around twice as labour intensive per acre as food crops, hence if the ratio of land use is 9 : 1, the ratio of labour use would be 9 : 2. Over the past 15 years the output volume of the major cash crops in Tanzania has been roughly constant,[5] so that any increment of agricultural labour would have been available for food crops. Perhaps the best estimate of the change in the agricultural population is from the Censuses of 1967 and 1978. These show an increase in males working in agriculture of 18.8 per cent and of rural females aged over 15[6] of 23.4 per cent—a total increase in the agricultural labour force of 21.4 per cent. Because all of this extra labour went into food crops, if, as we have suggested, labour (as opposed to land) is the major constraint upon crop output, food crop output would have risen by more than this, but not by much more. To be precise, if food output rose with the food labour force it must have increased by 26.9 per cent from 1967–78.[7] But over this period the national population increased by 42.5 per cent so that per capita food output on the above estimate declined by 11 per cent in 11 years. This would certainly help to explain the growing reliance upon food imports and food aid. It is, of course, possible that there were offsetting or compounding changes in yields per acre. The shift from cash to food crops, however, can have had only a marginal alleviating effect. On the above estimates, it added about 5 per cent to food production over a decade. Furthermore, with so little land remaining under cash crops, the scope for feeding the ever-growing urban population by further diversion of labour from cash crops is strictly limited. If Tanzania is to be self-sufficient in food, either labour productivity in growing food crops must rise, or the growth of the urban population must be reduced to no more than match that of the labour force in food production. Over the period 1967–78, while the food labour force grew by around 27 per cent the population of Dar es Salaam grew by around 180 per cent.

We will return to the analysis of crop production in more detail when we discuss peasant differentiation in Chapter 4. We now turn to the second component of household income, livestock.

Livestock income

Livestock income is often a highly problematic component of budget surveys because of the mixture of regular outputs (such as milk), sustainable offtake of the herd, and changes in the asset value of the herd. Furthermore, owing to very large annual fluctuations, correctly measured current livestock income is a poor guide to 'permanent livestock income'. The scale of the problem is discussed in the *Kenyan Integrated Rural Survey I* (Nairobi, Central Bureau of Statistics, 1977), which indicated that some 20 per cent of households surveyed ended up with a *negative farm income* for the year, almost entirely due to the effect of estimation of livestock income. These households had, however, a higher level of consumption than any other income group and should not be confused with the genuinely poor.[8]

The definition of livestock income which we have adopted deliberately refrains from using as a component the change in livestock valuation over the year. This greatly reduces the extent of negative income cases at the cost of theoretically imperfect conceptualization of livestock income. We consider that in the treatment of livestock there is some conflict between the theoretically proper and the empirically reasonable. We include in income the value of livestock sold along with income from skins, milk, eggs, and the hiring-out of livestock, minus costs incurred (excluding own labour). In addition, we value subsistence consumption of livestock, and livestock given away as bride price. Value is assigned to these units of livestock using the mean price of livestock sold. That is, we adopt the second procedure described in our above discussion of subsistence crop income for subsistence consumption of livestock because the objection raised to this procedure for food valuation seems less compelling in the case of livestock.

As defined, a little over three-quarters of all households had a non-zero net income from livestock, the mean for these households being 1,059 shillings per annum. A few households had costs in excess of income, the heaviest loss from livestock being 720 shillings.

Non-farming earnings

Non-farm income came from a wide variety of activities and occupations as can be gathered from the analysis of labour allocation earlier in the chapter. Since these activities generally involved small cell sizes it was considered more appropriate for most purposes to group all these earnings together into the single component, non-farm earnings. All surveyed households reported some labour input into activities other than in their own shamba, this often being work on the communal shamba. When we turn to peasant differentiation, we will find that there are indeed very wide differences in the remuneration of non-farm labour. However, taking an average over all households, mean earnings per annum from this source were 760 shillings.

Remittances received

In some African economies remittances received from urban relatives form a considerable component of peasant income. For example, in Kenya around 10 per cent of peasant income is accounted for in this way.[9] We have already seen, however, from Table 3.4 that relatively few Tanzanian peasant households have relatives working in urban areas, in fact fewer than 20 per cent. Not all these households received any remittances, for only 8 per cent of households had received cash or goods in the previous year. For these households, mean receipts were fairly high at 1,886 shillings, but because they were few in number, remittances formed only a small component (4 per cent) of aggregate peasant income, less than half the share of peasant income from this source in Kenya.

Total household income

Taking the sum of the above five components of income we arrive at total household income. Mean total household income was 3,892 shillings per annum, of which a little over half came from crops. The

Table 3.17: The composition of household income

	(per cent)
Net income from crop sales	14.1
Subsistence crop consumption	41.4
Net livestock income	21.0
Non-farm earnings	19.5
Remittances	4.0
Total	100.0

share of each income component is shown in Table 3.17. The calculation both of total income and of the shares of the various components is dependent upon the concepts and methods adopted. For example, to value crop production at urban instead of rural prices would have inflated both total income and the crop component. This makes comparison with other data sources and income estimates difficult. In particular, comparison with earlier household budget surveys is not possible because they sampled different populations and used methods and concepts which are often not fully reported and may be substantially different from our own. It is, however, useful to check our results against the estimates of informed users of the available macro-data. Probably, the most reliable of such estimates is that made by Livingstone (1982).[10] Livingstone estimated that in 1980 mean food consumption in the peasant household was around 4,850 shillings per annum and cash income, excluding livestock and remittances, was 1,080 shillings. Livingstone's estimate of food consumption was at urban prices, namely 2.50 shillings per kilo of maize against our rural price of 1.20 shillings. Deflating to the rural price level, his estimate is therefore around 2,330 shillings. We have no comparable estimate, as we only identify that sub-set of food consumption which is subsistence production. This we estimated at around 1,640 shillings at rural prices. For both figures to be correct would imply that 30 per cent of food was purchased, which is probably rather above what would be expected. However, both figures, far from being correct, are mere approximations subject to considerable error. The two estimates are sufficiently compatible not to be wholly implausible—which is as much as can be expected of Tanzanian food crop data at present. Livingstone's estimate of a sub-set of peasant cash income as 1,080 shillings is very close to our own estimate of the same sub-set, namely 1,053 shillings. The reader should not be deceived by this compatibility of the micro- and macro-data sources, for both are fragile. The macro-data, however, clearly lend some support to the micro-data. We will suggest in Chapter 4 that the internal coherence of the survey data constitutes a further ground for regarding the micro-data as being reliable.

Finally, it is useful to identify gross cash income. This is defined as total income minus subsistence crop income, minus own consumption and gifts of livestock, plus costs of crop production. The mean of gross cash income was 2,026 shillings per annum. The ratio of gross cash income to total income is virtually the same as that reported in the 1969 Household Budget Survey for rural households. This may be the result of a genuine shift into subsistence production offset by a change in survey methodology. However, it should caution against over-hasty acceptance of the thesis that peasants have retreated into subsistence production.

A profile of village households: a summary

This chapter has provided a profile of the demography, migration, employment, assets, and income of the typical peasant household in Tanzania. What we conclude is that such a household actually has rather few members, despite the notion of the 'extended family'. Owing to massive education and adult literacy programmes most people in the household are likely to be literate, but despite a model rural health programme the state of child health is very poor. The household is likely to be socially and economically isolated, with few households having present or former members who have worked or married outside the village. Work within the village is predominantly concentrated upon agriculture, either on the peasant's own shamba or on the communal holding. Thus the household, isolated from the wider economy, is confined to a very narrow range of employment activities. This narrow range of activity is reflected in the narrow range of assets held. Indeed, most households could be described as having effectively no productive assets since land is often sufficiently abundant to have little value and most households own no livestock beyond a few chickens. The income level generated by this configuration of limited activities and limited assets is, not unexpectedly, low and its composition is predominantly agricultural. Thus the typical household is very poor and has only the limited education of its members as an asset which might be exploited to raise standards of health and diversify the opportunities for its labour resources to generate a higher standard of living.

However, the 'typical' household is a statistical figment, as we are about to demonstrate.

Notes

1. R. H. Sabot, *Economic Development and Urban Migration: Tanzania 1900–1971* (Oxford, Clarendon Press, 1979); P. Collier, 'Migration and unemployment: A dynamic general equilibrium analysis applied to Tanzania', *Oxford Economic Papers*, 3, 1979.
2. D. Ghai and S. Radwan (eds.), *Agrarian Policies and Rural Poverty in Africa* (Geneva, ILO, 1983), Ch. 1.
3. As of 1983 inter-regional movement of 500 kg. packages has been allowed.
4. For a recent analysis of the Tanzanian rural marketing system, see M. Guerreiro, 'The structure and performance of agricultural marketing in Kenya and Tanzania and its impact upon rural–urban terms of trade and agricultural production' M.Lit. thesis, Oxford, 1984.
5. Ibid.
6. Females stating they work in agriculture is an unreliable proxy for the female agricultural population because of the conceptual confusions surrounding 'housewife' in peasant societies. Women may describe their occupation as 'housewife' and yet perform agricultural work, for such work is regarded as part of the normal duties of the peasant housewife.
7. If in 1978 labour was used in the ratio 9 : 2 on producing food and cash crops, then normalizing on these figures, the total labour force was 11 in 1978 and 9.09 in 1968. The cash crop labour force was constant at 2 so the food crop labour force grew from 7.09 to 9, an increase of 26.9 per cent.
8. See P. Collier and D. Lal, *Labour and Poverty in Kenya* (Oxford, Oxford University Press, 1986). Ch. 8.
9. See Republic of Kenya, Ministry of Finance and Planning, Central Bureau of Statistics, *Integrated Rural Survey, 1974–75: Basic Report* (Nairobi, Government Printer, 1977).
10. ILO, Jobs and Skills Programme for Africa, *Basic Needs in Danger: A Basic Needs Oriented Development Strategy for Tanzania* (Addis Ababa, JASPA, 1982).

4

Peasant Differentiation

In Chapter 3, we focused primarily upon a profile of the typical household. In many peasant societies, however, there is considerable differentiation—that is, inequality—in living standards. Though the 'typical' household, as profiled in Chapter 3, is clearly poor, it may be that rather few households in practice coincide with that profile, the typical merely being the statistical average taken from a group of households that is very poor and another that is relatively rich. This chapter seeks first to quantify and then to explain rural differentiation. The quantification of differentiation requires a measure which reasonable describes the relative living standard of a household, that is, one which ranks the economic well-being of households roughly as they would rank themselves. This is in fact quite a difficult task, and our approach is described in the next section.

There are many possible explanations of rural differentiation. In a complex risky environment, such as peasant agriculture, differences in luck and in judgement might well generate considerable differences in the income earned in a single year, which is all we observe. Most of such differences would be only temporary as luck or judgement changed. Alternatively, the observed differences in income might reflect permanent differences in well-being. This is likely to be the case if income differences are largely explicable in terms of differences in the assets with which households are endowed. The core of this chapter is therefore an investigation of the extent to which income differences can be functionally related to the differences in the endowment of assets. This issue is important because of its implications for policies directed towards the alleviation of poverty. Many studies have suggested that, in the absence of policy interventions, general economic development in very low income countries will only marginally improve the living standards of the poorest sections of the population. Yet, if specific policies are needed to aid the poor, it is not a priori clear how such policies should be designed. If rural inequalities are small, then generalized assistance to the rural population will suffice. If they are large but result from random shocks, then insurance schemes may be the most appropriate intervention. If inequalities are large and reflect permanent differences in the distribution of endowments then asset redistribution may be appropriate (this, of course, being a rationale for land reform in some countries). As this is the primary focus of the chapter, the analysis must rest upon a secure identification of poor and non-poor households. It is to this that we now turn.

The measurement of living standards

In the analysis of poverty and inequality, the first critical step is an appropriate measurement of living standards. This involves the definition of income and the specification of consumer units. We have already discussed the former; in particular, the use of calories instead of market prices to value subsistence food consumption reduces observed inequality and leads to a better identification of the poor. The specification of consumer units is also conceptually a highly complex issue. The two simple options—income per household or income per person—are both such a poor proxy for living standards that they are likely seriously to misidentify the poor. In particular, the former will show the poor to consist predominantly of small households, and the latter will show them to consist of large households composed mainly of young children. To improve upon these simple options we need to correct for differences in household composition.

Household composition differs between households in two distinct respects. First, children need less food than adults and females need less than males. We need, therefore, to identify types of member within a household. Secondly, with a given type of membership, some households are larger than others and benefit from economies of scale in consumption. There are two different approaches to correcting for composition. One is based on the nutritional requirements of typical individuals. The advantages of this approach are that it permits detailed disaggregation into many types and that it concerns food, which is the dominant component of expenditure. An example is given in Table 4.1. The disadvantage is that this type of information makes no correction for household size, thus ignoring economies of scale. The other approach, developed by Deaton and Muellbauer, is to compare the expenditure patterns of different types of household. Households of different composition are

Table 4.1: Calorie requirements by age and sex for East Africa

Age group	Sex	
	Male	Female
0–2	0.40	
3–4	0.48	
5–6	0.56	
7–8	0.64	
9–10	0.76	
11–12	0.80	0.88
13–14	1.00	1.00
15–18	1.20	1.00
19–59	1.00	0.88
60+	0.88	0.72

Source: Latham, op. cit., Appendix 1.

said to have common living standards when they reveal a common pattern of expenditure shares on various goods. This has the advantage of including the effects of economies of scale but the disadvantage of requiring enormous amounts of data for estimation. Engel curves have to be estimated separately for each different type of household. For example, to provide the level of disaggregation offered in Table 4.1 by the nutritional approach for ten groups of households would require 15 × 10 Engel curves. Since the estimation of each of these Engel curves would need a minimum of around 100 observations, the required sample size for the underlying household expenditure survey would have to be larger than that currently available. In the only practical application of the method in the context of less developed countries, Deaton simply disaggregated household members into adults and children and then concentrated on differences in household size.[1]

At the present time, then, corrections for household composition cannot be done precisely. We propose to splice together the two approaches, using the nutritional approach to correct for differences in type of member and the Deaton approach to correct for differences in household size. This has the advantage of retaining the detailed disaggregation of the nutritional approach, while making some attempt at taking economies of scale into account. It has the disadvantage of being a hybrid with insecure theoretical foundations.

The nutritional weights we adopt are those set out in Table 4.1. We infer economies of scale from Deaton's data on the scale factors to be applied for adult-only households as their size changes from a single member up to five members.[2] The scale factors are, directly, the average costs of a household of a particular size relative to those of a single member household. Implicitly, the change in average costs reflects a change in marginal costs. Deaton does not calculate scale factors for households of more than five adults, and since we need scale effects for households which are larger than these, we assumed that the marginal cost of subsequent units is the same as that of the fifth unit. The resulting average and marginal costs of additional members are set out in Table 4.2. Potentially, these scale factors differ for different income levels, but in Deaton's data, the alteration between income levels was small. Income changes altered more powerfully the adult/child conversion in Deaton's case study, but we see no way of incorporating this into Table 4.1.

Our resulting household composition correction factors are therefore estimated in two steps.

(a) Each member is assigned his/her appropriate adult equivalent weight from Table 4.1. These weights are then summed over all the members of the household. The result is the household measured in adult equivalent units (AEU).

Table 4.2: Household economies of scale

Household size (number of adults)	Marginal cost	Average cost
1	1.0	1.0
2	0.892	0.946
3	0.798	0.897
4	0.713	0.851
5	0.632	0.807
6	0.632	0.778
7	0.632	0.757
8	0.632	0.741
9	0.632	0.729
10+	0.632	0.719

(*b*)   The resulting size of the household in adult equivalent units is then multiplied by the average cost factor for a household with that many adults. The result is the household measured in adult equivalent units which have been adjusted to allow for economies of scale (adjusted adult equivalent units, AAEU).[3]

This measurement can then be used to divide total household income, yielding income per AAEU. This measure is a more appropriate indicator of the living standard of a household than is total household income, income per capita, or income per adult equivalent unit. Its purpose is to achieve a broadly correct identification of households which could properly be considered relatively poor or relatively rich.

Having arrived at a measure of living standards, it is now possible to quantify the extent of inequality. There are many summary statistical measures of inequality, but few of these are readily decomposable. Decomposability is important for our purpose since we wish to distinguish between ecological and economic components of inequality. For these purposes the best single indicator of the extent of inequality is the Theil Index,[4] which has several advantages over the rather better-known Gini coefficient, including ease of decomposition. Defined in terms of the distribution of income per AAEU over households, overall inequality as measured by the Theil Index was 0.40. This is a fairly high level of rural inequality, though it is below levels prevailing in Asia.

Given the emphasis in Tanzanian policy upon the village as a unit of resource sharing and accumulation, together with wide variations in ecological conditions, it might be expected that a considerable proportion of total inequality would be explained by differences between villages. In fact this was not the case: while there were quite large differences between some villages, only 16 per cent of total inequality was explained by inter-village inequality, the remaining 84 per cent being due to differences within villages. Although our sample of 20 villages might not be a true reflection of the extent of differences between the 8,000 villages in Tanzania, we consider that if anything our sample selection probably overstated differences. In stratifying by ecology, accessibility, and reputation, the survey possibly oversampled both relatively rich and relatively poor villages. If we reject the explanation that our sample of villages was atypically homogeneous, then either there is genuinely considerable inequality within villages despite the abundance of land or else the observed inequality is a consequence of erroneous data collection. The averages generated by our data may be consistent with other evidence, as we have seen, and yet the dispersion around those means may be misleading. For the moment, we will proceed on the assumption that our data do correctly describe the distribution of income. However, our analysis will indirectly impose internal consistency checks on our data, for we will be attempting to explain income differences in terms of other variables.

Given the above decomposition results, it follows that in studying the sources of inequality and relative poverty we must focus primarily not on ecological and geographic factors but on economic differentiation within the village. We begin our analysis of the nature of this differentiation by comparing the characteristics of the poorer 50 per cent of households with those of the better-off 50 per cent of households, ranking all households by their income per AAEU. We will describe these two groups as the poor and the non-poor. The cut-off level of income per AAEU which stratifies the population into these two groups, however, is only 800 shillings per year, and the mean income of the upper half of the population is only 1,935 shillings per AAEU, and 6,544 shillings per household. An income of some 820 shillings per annum is hardly adequate to raise a household above absolute poverty. Furthermore, the mean income of the lower half of the population was only 382 shillings per AAEU, and 1,294 shillings per household. We can certainly regard a mean household annual income of only $US160 as an indication of severe absolute poverty. Our reference to the two groups as the poor and the non-poor should therefore be seen as describing relative degrees of poverty and should not be interpreted as connoting one class of the near-destitute facing another class of kulaks.

Causes of poverty will be investigated by a sequence of levels of explanation. We start by analysing the links between poverty and particular sources of income. Is low income in a particular activity caused by low prices, or low quantities of output? To the extent that low income in an activity is due to low quantities of output rather than low prices, we need then to account for differences between households in quantities of output. The key question here is whether differences in output can be explained in terms of differences in the input of factor endowments, or are a reflection of differences in the returns on those endowments. We investigate this through the construction of production and earnings functions. A further potential source of income differences arises if rates of return on endowments differ between activities and some households are unable to gain access to the higher-return activities. We therefore investigate whether there are systematic differences in returns and whether poor households are concentrated in low-yielding activities.

From the above, the proximate causes of the lower incomes of the poor can be identified from among low prices for produce, a shortfall in particular endowments, misallocation of endowments to low-yielding activities, and low returns on endowments in particular activities. Each of these can be further investigated in terms of other characteristics. For example, if low prices were found to be a major proximate explanation of poverty, it would then be appropriate to investigate whether they could be explained in terms of low assets (suggesting an inability to store output to be sold at a time of favourable prices) or in terms of location. Similarly, low labour endowments might be explained in terms of disablement or past out-migration.

This then is our agenda for the analysis of differentiation. We begin by comparing the proportions of income from different sources received by the poor and the non-poor. Throughout the chapter, a central issue will be whether poverty is a common phenomenon generated by many disparate and unconnected causes or whether these causes are themselves so interrelated and cumulative that poverty can ultimately be traced to a limited number of processes.

Income differentiation by income component

Poor and non-poor households have radically different structures of income. Table 4.3 breaks down income for the two groups into the five previously discussed categories of income and also shows the proportion of households with a positive income from each source. Three-quarters of the income of poor households comes from crops, compared with half the income of non-poor households. Differences are even more marked, however, when crop income is divided into its subsistence and marketed components. Over 70 per cent of the poor group's income comes from subsistence crop income, which is double the share of income it constitutes for the non-poor. Conversely, the non-poor have higher income shares from all the other income sources—marketed crops, livestock, remittances, and non-farm income. This striking difference in income sources has powerful

Table 4.3: Income differentiation by income source

Source of income	All households			Poor households			Non-poor households		
	Percentage of households with positive income from source	Mean income per AAEU of households with positive income from source (sh.)	Percentage of total income	Percentage of households with positive income from source	Mean income per AAEU of households with positive income from source (sh.)	Percentage of total income	Percentage of households with positive income from source	Mean income per AAEU of households with positive income from source (sh.)	Percentage of total income
Crop income	98.1	630.5	53.8	98.7	289.5	74.7	97.6	982.1	49.5
(a) Own consumption	95.6	497.5	41.3	95.7	284.4	71.2	95.6	715.2	35.3
(b) Net sales	93.1	145.8	12.4	98.7	13.8	3.6	97.6	281.9	14.2
Livestock income	77.3	279.8	18.8	77.0	70.8	14.3	77.6	491.5	19.7
Remittances	8.2	598.6	4.3	2.7	290.7	2.0	13.9	658.7	4.7
Non-farm income	27.4	972.3	23.1	18.3	188.1	9.0	36.7	1 371.5	26.0
Total	100.0	1 151	100.0	100.0	382.4	100.0	100.0	1 935.6	100.0

implications for understanding the nature of rural poverty in Tanzania. The poor are heavily reliant upon subsistence income, and those who rely heavily on subsistence income are predominantly poor. Rural poverty does not appear to be a consequence of unfavourable or exploitative integration into market processes but instead stems primarily from the lack of integration into such processes. This has serious implications for the efficacy of past rural development policies which have tended to reduce peasant involvement in markets. This has come about partly through the severe decline in crop prices paid to peasants, partly through the institutional changes in crop marketing with the abolition of peasant cooperatives and their replacement with monopoly bureaucracies (a change now in part reversed), and partly also through the deterioration in rural transport. It is not clear whether there has been a marked shift towards subsistence cultivation or whether there has been a shift towards leisure, but it is clear from macro-data that there has been no general spreading of market opportunities.

Focusing on the non-subsistence income sources, the absolute differences in income per AAEU are enormous. Income from crop sales is 20 times higher for the non-poor than for the poor, non-farm income 15 times higher, remittances 12 times higher, and livestock 7 times higher. In the case of remittances and non-farm incomes, this is a compound of a difference in the incidence of those with some income from the source and a difference in the mean level of income. Among the non-poor, approximately twice as many households have access to these income sources. In the case of livestock, the incidence of those with some income is the same for the two groups of households; income differences cannot be explained by the ownership of livestock. However, livestock is a broad aggregate which includes chickens along with oxen so that there might well be substantial differences in the type of livestock owned. This will be explored subsequently.

We now turn to correlations between income sources. Approximately half of overall income is from crops and half from non-crops. Is an atypically low crop income offset by high non-crop income or is it compounded by low non-crop income? A simple correlation of the two income sources is inappropriate because the relationship between the two is not monotonic. In particular, those households with zero crop income have very high non-crop income, mainly from wages. Only 14 households had zero crop income but they had a mean income per AAEU of some 150 per cent above the mean for all households, their mean non-crop income being five times the average for all households. Therefore, for this group, crop and non-crop income offset each other. By contrast, for those with positive crop income, crop and non-crop income are positively related. The proportion of total income contributed by crop income does not vary significantly with the level of crop income. Low crop income is associated with proportionately low non-crop income.

To conclude, there appears to be a small village élite not closely integrated into agriculture. Among households cultivating land, though, farm and non-farm income are positively correlated. This is a further reflection of the previously identified link between subsistence income and poverty. We have suggested that the low income which the poor derive from market sources is an indication of their lack of participation in markets. Strictly, this is at present only one possible interpretation of the data. An alternative interpretation is that the poor do participate, but on such unfavourable terms, getting atypically low prices for their produce, that they generate little income. We now investigate this latter interpretation.

Income differences due to price differences

The income gap between poor and non-poor households is some 770 shillings per annum per AAEU. Table 4.3 showed that differences in crop sales account for 18 per cent of this gap and differences in livestock income account for 21 per cent. Hence, if we can explain the differences in these two income sources we have accounted for a substantial amount of overall income inequality. For each of these two income sources, incomes can differ for three distinct reasons. First, the poor might sell the same quantities as the non-poor but receive lower prices for their output. This is known to be one aspect of inequality among peasants in Nigeria, for example. Because of high storage costs, grain prices are low after harvest and rise sharply through the year until the next harvest. Poor peasants, often in debt, tend to sell their crop immediately after harvest and thus get lower prices than those who can afford to store their crop. In Tanzania storage costs of grain are probably very high due to losses through insects. Although the official maize price does not vary through the year, the unofficial price appears—on the scanty evidence available—to be perhaps 60 per cent higher before the harvest than after.

There are, however, substantial differences between Tanzania and Nigeria. Peasants do not generally sell their grain and then buy some of it back for their own consumption (as is done in Nigeria), except in the coastal and Dodoma areas. Because of the unreliability of rural grain markets in Tanzania, even poor households attempt to store most of the grain they will need for their own consumption. Conversely, because storage is severely limited, richer households cannot generally store sufficiently large quantities of grain to make significant sales in the pre-harvest period. There is therefore little reason to expect price differences to be an important contributor to income differences.

A second possible reason for differences in income is differences in the costs of production. Poor and non-poor households may sell the same quantities of output and get the same prices but incur different levels of cash costs and hence generate different net incomes. Large differences in costs might reflect either differences in technology or differences in farming ability.

The last reason for differences in income is, of course, differences in the quantity of sales. These differences can in turn be broken down into a difference in the incidence of households entering the market and differences in the mean quantity of sales of those in the market. We now break down income differences into price, cost, and quantity components, taking first income from crop sales.

The measured weighted average of crop prices creates a potential index number problem. When the quantities sold by poor households are valued at the mean prices attained by non-poor households, the value of sales is 9 per cent greater than when sales are valued at prices actually received by poor households. Potentially, the value of non-poor households' sales at the prices received by the poor could be radically different from 9 per cent less than their actual value due to differences in weight by crop, but in fact this is not the case. Thus, the poor would have a 9 per cent greater income from crop sales if they received the prices paid to the non-poor. Hence price was not an important explanation of differences in income from crop sales.

There was no significant difference in the proportion of households reporting some production costs—91 per cent of the poor and 94 per cent of the non-poor. For those reporting costs, there was a substantial difference in the level of costs between the two groups, but since costs were 75 per cent higher for the non-poor than for the poor, we cannot use this to explain why the latter had low net income from crop sales. The remaining differences therefore, are the result of a lower quantity of sales.

The reason for poor households' selling less of their crops is accounted for by the greater incidence of households not selling any crops. Only 42 per cent of poor households made crop sales as opposed to 75 per cent of non-poor households. If the proportion of the poor making crop sales were the same as the non-poor, this would have raised the gross crop sales of the poor by 53 shillings per AAEU. This would have raised net crop income (assuming that there was no increase in costs) from 14 shillings to 67 shillings per AAEU. If, instead, the poor had achieved the prices of the non-poor, then gross crop sales per AAEU would have been 6 shillings greater, so that net sales would have been increased from 14 shillings to 20 shillings. If both the above adjustments are made together then net crop sales per AAEU would rise by 64 shillings. Since the total difference per AAEU was 262 shillings we may conclude that 76 per cent of this shortfall in the income of the poor was due to the lower mean quantities of crops sold even when sales were made. Of the remainder, a further 21 per cent was due to the lower proportion of households making any crop sales, and 3 per cent was accounted for by lower prices received for crops. Some 97 per cent of the shortfall in net crop sale income, which accounts for 18 per cent of the entire shortfall in income, can be explained by differences in quantities sold rather than in prices or crops. This analysis lead to the conclusion that the poor get less net income from crop sales because they sell fewer crops.

The same analysis is now applied to net livestock income. Here price differences are even less important, because on average the poor get slightly higher prices (10 per cent) than the non-poor. Nor are cost differences an explanation: proportionately fewer poor incur any livestock costs, and those who do incur lower mean costs than those incurred by the non-poor with livestock costs. The difference between the 54 shillings income per AAEU of the poor and the 381 shillings of the non-poor, therefore, must be wholly accounted for by quantities of livestock consumed and sold.

There was no significant difference in the proportion of total livestock income which was subsistence consumption, namely 58 per cent for the non-poor and 54 per cent for the poor. Nor was there any difference in the proportion of households getting *some* livestock income (77 per cent). Income differences were entirely explained by the lower quantities of livestock sold and consumed by those who had livestock.

To conclude, price and cost differences were unimportant for both crops and livestock. Yet between them, crops and livestock accounted for 65 per cent of differences in living standards (Table 4.4).

Table 4.4: The contribution of crops and livestock to income differentiation

Reason for different living standards	(per cent)
Crop consumption	26
Crop sales	18
Livestock consumption	12
Livestock sales	9
Total	65
These due to differences in:	
Price	0.5
Cost	0
Quantity	64.5

We may therefore reject as an explanation of poverty and inequality the thesis that the rural poor participate in commodity markets on unfavourable terms. Proximately, they are poor because they scarcely participate in commodity markets. Around 65 per cent of the income gap between poor and non-poor households can be explained in terms of a shortfall in the quantities of crops and livestock consumed and sold. Clearly, little is consumed and sold because little is produced. Why little is produced becomes our next question.

Functional links between incomes and endowments

We have now traced income inequalities to differences in quantities of crop and livestock output which, when taken together, explain 65 per cent of total income differences, leaving differences in non-farm earnings and remittances to account for the remaining 35 per cent. The next step in our analysis is to discover why differences in these quantities occur. Differences in non-farm earnings will also be examined in this section. First, we shall consider crop production.

Crop production

Differences in crop production will be analysed at two distinct levels of aggregation. First, for each of the major crops we investigate whether differences in the quantity of output produced can be functionally related to differences in inputs applied in the production process. Secondly, we investigate whether differences in total crop production can be explained by differences in the inputs used in crop production. This second level of analysis is important because even if there is a strong relationship between inputs and outputs for each specific crop, there may be only a weak relationship in aggregate if some farmers misallocate their resources by choosing a crop mix which generates a low value of output relative to their use of inputs.

Links between inputs and outputs by crop were assessed by estimating production functions for specific crops. At this level of disaggregation, no usable data were available on labour input. The independent variables taken were land acreage, the number of crops inter-cropped with the crop being considered, expenditure upon inputs (including imputed values for own-produced non-labour inputs), and the level of education of the household head. The latter was a means of controlling for education-induced differences in farming ability. Education was seldom significant and was dropped from equations in which it was not significant. In addition, nineteen village dummy variables were introduced, all dummies taking the value zero except for that of the village to which the holding belonged. This corrected for major ecological variations between villages. After experimenting with CES (constant elasticity of substitution) forms it was found that the Cobb–Douglas function performed best, the underlying equation being:

$$Q = aL^b \cdot \left(\frac{1}{M}\right)^c \cdot e^{dE} \cdot e^{fl}$$

where

Q = Output of crop (kilos)
L = Land under crop (acres)
M = Number of other crops inter-cropped with crop + 1
E = Level of education of household head
  1 = none
  2 = adult literacy

3 = lower primary
4 = upper primary
5 = secondary
I = Inputs in shillings
a, b, c, d, f = constants

The regression was estimated in logarithmic form. The results of the nine usable crop-specific production functions are reported in Table 4.5.

Acreage, which was nearly always significant, had coefficients in the range 0.51 to 0.92. Since no control was made for labour input this coefficient represents the scale effect of increasing acreage combined with actual increases in labour input. Since the coefficient is always below unity we may interpret this either as diseconomies of scale or as indicating a less than proportionate increase in actual labour input as acreage increases. The coefficient on inter-cropping is more complex. If inter-cropping is inefficient then the coefficient on the number of crops inter-cropped will be greater than unity. For example, a coefficient of two would indicate that if two crops were inter-cropped together on one acre, then instead of generating the same output as half an acre of each crop grown separately, the equivalent single-cropped acreage would be equivalent to only a quarter of an acre of each crop. The observed coefficient of 1.03 on beans, not significantly different from unity, and of 0.52 on maize, suggests that the common maize–beans inter-cropping leads to gains in maize output without losses in the output of beans compared with single cropping half the area of each crop. If inter-cropping does not reduce output per acre at all, then the variable will not be significant. This would indicate that from an economic point of view inter-cropping was highly efficient. Therefore both a significant coefficient below unity and an insignificant coefficient imply that inter-cropping is efficient. This always seems to be the case with the nine crops considered. If this is correct, it suggests that the Government's agricultural extension efforts to discourage inter-cropping may have been misplaced.

In five cases inputs are significant. The coefficients range from 0.0013 to 0.0073 which implies that an expenditure of 100 shillings on inputs increases output by between 14 and 107 per cent. Education is significant only in some cases and is never highly significant. The coefficient ranges between 0.058 and 0.125, indicating that each of

Table 4.5: Crop-specific production functions

Crop	n	r^2	F	Land area	Inter-cropping	Inputs	Education
Maize	410	0.63	28.3	0.59[a] (8.8)[d]	0.52[a] (4.0)	0.0015[a] (3.4)	0.058[c] (1.6)
Sorghum	180	0.36	6.5	0.69[a] (5.8)	0.53[a] (2.8)	0.0010 (1.0)	—
Beans	156	0.61	15.5	0.63[a] (5.6)	1.03[a] (5.4)	0.0013[c] (1.9)	—
Cassava	104	0.63	9.8	0.77[a] (7.8)	0.06 (0.3)	0.0073[a] (3.0)	0.119[c] (1.9)
Bananas	95	0.77	30.9	0.12 (1.1)	−0.33 (1.3)	0.0014[b] (2.2)	0.119[b] (2.1)
Coffee	92	0.29	5.0	0.87[a] (4.5)	0.04 (0.1)	0.0017 (1.4)	0.129 (1.3)
Groundnuts	107	0.44	7.6	0.15 (1.0)	0.32 (1.0)	0.0022[b] (2.2)	0.125[c] (1.7)
Millet	100	0.48	12.2	0.51[a] (3.4)	−0.16 (−0.7)	0.0037 (1.5)	—
Cashew	16	0.50	4.0	0.92[b] (2.8)	0.25 (0.3)	—	—

[a] = significant at 1 per cent level.
[b] = significant at 5 per cent level.
[c] = significant at 10 per cent level.
[d] = figures in parentheses represent t-statistic.

the four education steps above zero, on average, raises output by between 7 per cent and 18 per cent of the level achieved by those with no education. Since the coefficient is barely significant, this result is difficult to interpret, although it is at least consistent with the hypothesis that the Government's investment in primary education and adult literacy has indirect benefits on agricultural production. This is consistent with Schultz's hypothesis and other studies on the contribution of education to farmer productivity.[5]

The second level of crop regression was based on gross crop output as the dependent variable. This was the sum of the value of own consumption estimated by means of calorie prices and the gross value of crop sales. Data on labour input per household were available for this regression. The underlying equation was the same as before but with Q reinterpreted and 'land' being the total acreage operated. The result was:

$$\log Q = 0.65 \log A + 0.08 \log N + 0.74E + 0.004I$$
$$\quad\quad (9.96) \quad\quad\quad (1.35) \quad\quad\quad (2.46) \quad (4.63)$$

$$n = 540$$
$$r^2 = 0.55$$
$$F = 27.9$$

where

$\quad$ A = land operated (acreage)
$\quad$ N = labour days worked on own shamba
$\quad$ ( ) = t-statistic.

The sum of the land and labour coefficients—0.73—suggests that farming was subject to diseconomies of scale. The coefficient on inputs implies that the addition to output contributed by the mean level of purchased inputs (99 shillings) for a household using the mean amount of land, labour, education, and own produced inputs (117 shillings) was 800 shillings. Superficially this suggests that many peasants face cash constraints, as this would account for the very high return on purchased inputs. However, such an inference must be heavily qualified. The form of production function which we have adopted, with inputs entering as an exponent, imposes increasing returns on inputs. This form was chosen as a means of handling the problem that many households recorded zero purchased inputs and some recorded zero total inputs, the valuation of own-produced inputs being difficult and rather arbitrary. Because of this unsatisfactory feature of the production function, the apparent marginal product of inputs will overstate the true marginal product. The addition to output contributed by the 99 shillings of purchased inputs would be only 500 shillings if own-produced inputs were treated as marginal inputs, as opposed to 800 shillings if purchased inputs were treated as marginal. The total return on purchased inputs thus appears to be between five and eight times their cost. This gives us no guide as to the contributions of the marginal shilling of expenditure which might even be less than its cost. However, with such a high average return it may indeed be the case that the marginal return is high, supporting the notion of a cash constraint.

The coefficient on education implies that, on average, each increment in education level raised the value of gross crop output by about 9 per cent, controlling for land, labour, and inputs. Thus, a household head who had completed primary education would produce around 27 per cent more output from given inputs than someone with no education. The education coefficient is more significant than in any of the crop-specific regressions (where in most cases it was significant). Perhaps the most likely interpretation of this is that education influences cropping choice by enabling farmers to evaluate the returns from alternative crops. It might also make them less prone to risk, partly by giving them some opportunities for access to non-farm wage income; or it might change their attitude to risk, making them less averse to taking risks. To conclude our analysis of crop production functions, the overall level of explanation achieved was quite high. The most powerful determinant of crop output was land, both at the level of specific crop acreages and at that of the total holding size operated. We may then safely infer that any substantial difference in mean holding size between the poor and the non-poor would give rise to substantial differences in crop output. We have established links between crop income and the endowments which generate that income. To determine whether overall differences in income between the poor and the non-poor can be traced back to differences in endowments, we must first establish such functional links for the other components of income. We now turn to livestock income.

Livestock production

The procedure applied to differences in crop income was also used in an attempt to explain differences in livestock income. Regressions for specific types of livestock were not estimated because endowments such as land could not be divided between different types. The regression was of gross livestock income (with sales valued at mean market prices) on the total value of livestock owned, land owned, livestock expenses, and the education of the household head. The result is stated below:

$$V = 0.062W^a + 79.5A^b + 1.58C^b + 113.0E$$
$$\quad\ (3.40) \qquad (2.05) \quad\ (2.43) \qquad (0.95)$$
$$n = 74$$
$$r^2 = 0.44$$
$$F = 2.76$$

where

V = gross livestock income (in shillings at mean market prices)
W = livestock wealth (shillings)
A = acres of land owned
C = livestock expenses (shillings)
E = education of household head
$(\ )$ = t-statistic
a = significant at 1 per cent level
b = significant at 5 per cent level.

Education is not significant in the regression. Possibly this is because improved ('exotic') breeds of livestock, which do require specialized care for successful rearing, are very rare, and nearly all livestock income is from native livestock which is resistant to disease and whose characteristics are well understood by peasants. The value of the herd is significant, the coefficient implying an offtake rate of 6.2 per cent per annum which is reasonable. Land is also significant, though at a lower level. Whether this is because land is needed for livestock or because it is another asset correlated with livestock cannot be determined. Finally, livestock inputs show a return of 1.6 shillings of output for each shilling of input.

We may conclude that livestock income is functionally related to endowments, in particular being strongly dependent upon the value of livestock owned.

Non-farm earnings

For non-farm earnings, a simple earnings function was estimated with age and education as the explanatory variables. Education was investigated through the inclusion of four dummy variables for adult literacy, lower primary, upper primary, and secondary schooling.

For a person with no education all four dummy variables were set at zero, while for a person with secondary schooling all four dummy variables were set at unity. Education, then, was treated as a hierarchy, with those progressing to higher levels not losing the benefits of the education they had received at lower levels of the hierarchy. Earnings were entered in log form, the regression results being:

$$\log Y = 2.99 + 0.076A - 0.28D_1 + 1.03D_2 + 1.05D_3 + 1.85D_4$$
$$\quad\ (2.65)\ (2.57)\quad (-0.88)\quad (3.29)\quad (3.97)\quad (2.45)$$

$$n = 239$$
$$r^2 = 0.22$$
$$F = 13.0$$

where

Y = non-farm earnings (shillings per annum)
A = age (years)
D_1 = adult literacy dummy (unity if adult literacy or higher)
D_2 = lower primary dummy (unity if lower primary or higher)
D_3 = upper primary dummy (unity if upper primary or higher)
D_4 = secondary dummy (unity if secondary education).

Though adult literacy was insignificant, the three levels of formal schooling were highly significant in explaining the earnings of the 239 workers covered by the regression. Having lower primary education doubled earnings from the baseline of the uneducated. Upper primary education further tripled earnings, and secondary education raised earnings by six times more. Since a person with secondary education also benefits from the effects of the lower levels of education he has acquired, his non-farm earnings are nearly 40 times those of an uneducated person with non-farm earnings. The contribution of education to non-farm earnings (for those with such earnings) is shown for a representative person aged 35 in Table 4.6.

Higher earnings, as a result of education, could be a result of higher wage rates per day, or of access to non-farm employment in the first place. All the people in our sample who were included in our previous regression had worked for some days on activities other than their own shamba, but we had not accounted for days worked. We now account for days worked in non-farm employment, excluding the work on the communal farm and other shambas that did not merit remuneration. Only 89 workers fall into the category of having

Table 4.6: Non-farm earnings by education for a person aged 35 with positive earnings

Education	Earnings (sh. p. a.)
None	284
Adult literacy	215
Lower primary	602
Completed primary	1 720
Secondary	10 938

worked in non-farm employment. For this group we repeated the earnings function, now accounting for days worked. The results are set out below:

$$\log Y = 4.59 + 0.45A - 0.19D_1 + 0.86D_2 + 0.43D_3 + 0.27D_4 + 0.01W$$
$$ (2.62)\ \ (1.1)\ \ (-0.39)\quad (1.82)\quad (1.26)\quad (0.35)\quad (6.11)$$

$$n = 89$$
$$r^2 = 0.46$$
$$F = 10.0$$

where W = days worked on non-farm activities.

Among these workers, education is not significant as an explanation of earnings, days worked being the most important variable. This suggests that education is important in our previous regression principally because it rations access to the remunerative subset of non-shamba employment, rather than determining differences within such employment.

The determinants of access to non-farm wage employment were investigated using logit analysis. This estimates the probability of a member of the labour force with particular characteristics holding non-farm wage employment. The results are set out below:

$$\log\left(\frac{p}{1-P}\right) = \ 0.93 + 0.77D_1 + 0.52D_2 + 0.77D_3 + 1.86D_4 - 1.74S$$
$$\phantom{\log\left(\frac{p}{1-P}\right) =} (1.38)\ \ (0.44)\quad (0.36)\quad (0.27)\quad (0.66)\quad (0.28)$$
$$\phantom{\log\left(\frac{p}{1-P}\right) =} [0.43]\ \ [3.09]\quad [2.11]\quad [8.23]\quad [7.65]\quad [37.77]$$

$$\phantom{\log\left(\frac{p}{1-P}\right) =} -0.03A - 36.65\frac{1}{A}$$
$$\phantom{\log\left(\frac{p}{1-P}\right) =} (0.28)\quad (20.92)$$
$$\phantom{\log\left(\frac{p}{1-P}\right) =} [2.52]\quad\ \ [3.07]$$

Fraction of concordant pairs 0.80

$$n = 1334$$

where

　　p = the probability of employment
　　S = gender dummy (male = 1, female = 2)
　　( ) = standard error
　　[ ] = chi-square values.

Secondary and completed primary education are indeed highly significant determinants of access to wage employment, as is gender. The effect of age is not monotonic: as might be expected, the probability of access to a wage job first rises with age and then declines, peaking at 36 years. In Table 4.7 are set out the probabilities of access as they vary by characteristics. Thus, a thirty-six-year-old man with secondary education has a three-in-four chance (p = 0.74) of a wage job while a woman of the same age who has attended only

Table 4.7: Access to non-farm wage employment

Age	Education	Probability of gaining employment	
		Males	Females
15	none	0.022	0.004
36	none	0.054	0.010
36	adult literacy	0.110	0.021
36	primary standards 1–4	0.172	0.035
36	primary standards 5–8	0.310	0.073
36	secondary	0.742	0.336

adult literacy classes has a one-in-fifty chance. A woman with secondary education who is in the labour force has about the same chance of wage employment as a man with primary education. Again education is a powerful source of differentiation, for it displays increasing returns. The first four years of education raise a man's chance of a job by 0.12, the next four by 0.14, and the final four by 0.43.

　　To conclude, we have again established a link between an income component and the endowment which generates it, in this case non-shamba earnings being dependent principally upon education and gender.

Income differentiation and endowment differentiation

We now consider the extent to which differences in incomes between the poor and the non-poor can be explained by differences in endowments. First, we identify the extent of differences in endowments. For this purpose we revert to the concept of adjusted adult equivalent units (AAEU), all endowments being expressed per AAEU, as were income components.

Endowment differentiation

Total land owned differed significantly, but not greatly, between the poor and the non-poor. Per AAEU the former owned 1.40 acres and the latter 1.67 acres, this being around 20 per cent more. There were also some differences in the cropping pattern of these acreages. Table 4.8 sets out these differences for 12 major crops and three groups of crop. The first crop group is basic foods. It is noticeable that the poor, even though overall they have 20 per cent less acreage, actually grow nearly 20 per cent more acreage of cassava per AAEU. Cassava is the principal famine crop, not highly regarded for taste but a standby for necessity. Cassava, in the terminology of consumer theory, is an 'inferior' good, so we would expect the poor to devote a larger acreage to it. The fact that this is indeed what we find suggests that our identification of the poor has been accurate. Overall, the non-poor have 9 per cent more acreage of basic food crops than the poor. Particularly striking is the large difference in bean acreage. Beans are almost entirely grown by inter-cropping with maize and it appears that the poor have been less able either to perceive or to implement the benefits of inter-cropping their maize with beans which we elicited from our crop-specific production functions.

The second crop group is of identifiable cash crops such as coffee and sesame. The proportion of their land which the non-poor devote to these crops is double that of the poor, which amounts to two and a half times the mean acreage per AAEU of the poor. The remaining crops are grown proportionately by the two income classes. Since the cash crops can be expected on average to yield higher returns, the difference in land use is significant. It suggests that the non-poor have chosen to grow cash crops either because they have more land and so can still grow enough of the basic foods, or because they have higher incomes and so can afford to take the risk of growing cash crops instead of food crops. Regressing the proportion of land

Labour and Poverty

Table 4.8: Land use by income class

Crop	Land use (acres)	
	Poor	Non-poor
Basic foods		
Maize	0.50	0.49
Millet	0.10	0.14
Sorghum	0.15	0.17
Beans	0.06	0.11
Cassava	0.13	0.07
Groundnuts	0.06	0.07
Total	1.00	1.09
Proportion of all land	71.5%	65.6%
Cash crops		
Coffee	0.039	0.123
Sunflower	0.000	0.007
Sugar cane	0.001	0.006
Tobacco	0.007	0.002
Sesame	0.002	0.007
Cashew nuts	0.015	0.021
Total	0.064	0.166
Proportion of all land	4.6%	9.9%
Other crops	0.334	0.409
Proportion of all land	23.9%	24.5%

devoted to the cash crops of the second group on total holding size and on income per AAEU, we find that although the coefficients upon both terms are positive, the former is not significant, income being significant at the 5 per cent level. The regression analysis, then tends to support the second reason for the observed relationship, with income rather than land playing the critical role.

In addition to differences in the total amount of land owned and the cropping pattern of that land, there are very large differences in the ownership of livestock. Valuing all livestock at mean market prices, the poor own only 309 shillings of livestock per AAEU, while the non-poor own 2,254 shillings of livestock. It is apparent that livestock is a far more differentiated asset than land. This is not surprising: before villagization, land was sometimes freely available and since villagization there have been tight controls on land transactions. Hence, land is unlikely to be the principal channel of asset accumulation. By contrast, livestock has never been a free good and its accumulation is still unregulated.

We now consider differences in labour endowments. This is of considerable importance for the formulation of poverty policy. If the poor have very little labour then there is little opportunity of significantly increasing their incomes through higher earnings and raised output. In such circumstances, the poor must either be given transfer payments, which in Tanzania would be difficult to administer, or be given access to publicly provided goods. If, however, the poor have substantial labour endowments then policy aimed at alleviating poverty should try to create an environment in which the poor are able to earn higher incomes.

We find no difference in the number of labour force members per AAEU between the poor (0.72 members per AAEU) and the non-poor (0.73 members per AAEU). Neither is there a significant difference between total days worked per worker (218 and 226 days respectively) so that per AAEU there is only a 5 per cent difference between the number of days worked (157 days as opposed to 165). We can immediately reject the hypothesis that the cause of poverty is a high dependency ratio: the poor do almost as much work as the non-poor. However, the latter earn some 406 per cent more per AAEU than the former, of which only 5 per cent is accounted for by quantity of work; the rest is attributable to different rates of return for work. This supports our reasons for constructing the concept 'AAEU', for had we identified the poor by means of per capita or total household income, the resultant 'poor' would have appeared to have a much higher dependency ratio, and this would have obscured the true causes of poverty.

Although there is virtually no difference between poor and non-poor as regards the total quantity of work there is a difference in the composition of work. For both groups, total labour input in their own shamba per AAEU is almost the same—at 102 days and 105 days respectively. Note that although the poor put in fewer days, they have less land, so days per acre are higher for the poor than for the non-poor. Days worked per AAEU on the communal shamba are, however, very varied, the mean for the poor being 44 days per annum against only 34 days for the non-poor. Since this is an important result it is worth investigating it in connection with another part of the questionnaire. The survey enquired not only about annual labour allocation but also about activities during the busy season. Here, the reference periods were days per week and hours per day, so that we can compare the number of hours per week worked per AAEU during the busy season on the communal shamba. For the poor the mean is 5.76 hours and for the non-poor 4.54 hours per week. Thus the section of the questionnaire which investigated days per year is corroborated by the section which investigated hours per week during the busy season. In the first case the poor contributed 29 per cent more labour to the communal shamba while in the latter they contributed 27 per cent more. In Chapter 3 we observed that work on the communal shamba was evenly spread through the year. We conclude that the observed difference in labour input on the communal shamba is a major finding of the survey.

This difference is offset by work related neither to the communal shamba nor to that of the household. The poor work only 11 days per AAEU on such activities, as opposed to 26 days for the non-poor. For the busy season we can break this down into working for wages and working for own business. Interestingly enough, while the poor work per AAEU only 30 per cent as many days for wages they work nearly 60 per cent more days than the non-poor on their own businesses. It is, therefore, access to wage employment opportunities which is the differentiating factor. Work on their own business is negatively related to differentiation. Apparently, the poor have few productive outlets for their labour. They devote more working days per acre on their own shambas though these are planted with less remunerative crops, they work more days on communal shambas—usually for low returns, and more days on their own businesses. We shall see that the poor also receive drastically lower returns from working on their businesses than do the non-poor. The poor then appear to be forced into a range of low-income activities, including marginal enterprises.

The greater number of days worked off-shamba by the non-poor is matched by a difference in occupational structure. Only 4 per cent of the poor, compared with 11 per cent of the non-poor, have a principal occupation other than farmer.

We turn next to differences in education. The data are presented in Table 4.9. It can be seen that as regards the labour force as a whole, and household heads in particular, the poor have systematically lower educational attainments. Assigning arbitrary weights to

Table 4.9: Education by income class

Education	Household heads		All labour force	
	Poor	Non-poor	Poor	Non-poor
None	110[a]	75	265	218
	(59)	(41)	(55)	(45)
Adult literacy	65	50	125	126
	(57)	(43)	(50)	(50)
Lower primary	82	98	142	166
	(46)	(54)	(46)	(54)
Upper primary	43	58	113	167
	(43)	(57)	(40)	(60)
Secondary	1	8	2	10
	(11)	(89)	(17)	(83)

[a] The upper figure in each cell refers to the number of poor or non-poor and the lower figure in parentheses to their percentage shares.

the various levels of education—unity to adult literacy, two to lower primary, three to upper primary, and four to secondary education—the heads of non-poor households have on average 30 per cent more education than the heads of poor households. Of course, the figure of 30 per cent is dependent upon the weights used. A less arbitrary quantification can be made by using the coefficients from the previously estimated logit function of access to wage employment. Were heads of both poor and non-poor households all thirty-six-year-old males, so that the only difference in characteristics was in education, the heads of non-poor households would have had a 0.174 chance of access to wage employment, compared with a 0.137 chance for heads of poor households. Thus, the heads of non-poor households would have had a 27 per cent greater chance of access to wage employment.

The overall differences in endowments between poor and non-poor households are summarized in Table 4.10. Those endowments which stand out as being distinctly differentiated are livestock, access to wage employment, and the acreage of cash crops. Two activities are strongly differentiated in favour of the poor, namely, time spent working on an own-business and time spent working on the communal shamba. In the conditions prevailing in the rural areas, entrepreneurs are predominantly poor while wage-earners

Table 4.10: Endowments of poor and non-poor households per AAEU

Endowment	Poor	Non-poor	Non-poor/poor
Land (acres)	1.40	1.57	1.19
of which: basic foods	1.00	1.09	1.09
cash crops	0.06	0.17	2.80
Livestock (sh.)	309	2 254	7.29
Labour force members	0.72	0.73	1.01
Days worked	218	225	1.04
of which: own shamba	102	105	1.03
communal shamba	44	34	0.77
own business[a]	1.00	0.62	0.62
wages[a]	1.00	3.30	3.30
Education of household head[b]	1.20	1.56	1.30

[a] Normalized on the poor.

[b] No education = 0, adult literacy = 1, lower primary = 2, upper primary = 3, secondary = 4.

are predominantly non-poor. While this might not coincide with certain preconceptions of patterns of inequality, it is quite apparent from the data. We will return to this issue in our final chapter.

Endowment concentration

We now investigate whether the above differences in endowments are offsetting or cumulative; that is, are households which are poorly endowed with one asset also poorly endowed with others? Table 4.11 presents the correlation matrix between various endowments. The labour force per AAEU and land per AAEU are both positively and significantly correlated with all other endowments except mean educational attainment, where there is a negative correlation. Livestock wealth is positively and significantly correlated only with land and the number of workers. The educational level of the labour force is significantly and negatively correlated with land and livestock wealth. Finally, the ownership of a business is significantly and positively correlated with land and labour endowments. However, correlation might be dominated by intra-group relationships rather than by differences between the poor and the non-poor. As a guide to the characteristics of poverty, we therefore repeat the procedure used to analyse the concentration of income components. For each

Table 4.11: *Endowment correlation matrix*

	Land	Livestock wealth	Labour force	Days worked	Education of labour force	Business ownership
Land	1.000 (0.000)ᵃ 590					
Livestock wealth	0.113 (0.017) 443	1.000 (0.000) 446				
Labour force	0.313 (0.001) 590	0.115 (0.015) 446	1.000 (0.000) 594			
Days worked	0.275 (0.001) 590	0.021 (0.654) 446	0.691 (0.001) 594	1.000 (0.000) 594		
Education of labour force	-0.144 (0.001) 588	-0.218 (0.001) 443	-0.056 (0.173) 591	-0.051 (0.209) 591	1.000 (0.000) 591	
Business ownership	0.106 (0.010) 590	0.009 (0.854) 446	0.165 (0.001) 594	0.121 (0.003) 594	0.024 (0.559) 591	1.000 (0.000) 594

ᵃ Terms in parentheses are levels of significance. Bottom term is n.

endowment we calculate the means of other endowments owned for the more well-endowed and the less well-endowed groups.

Dividing households equally on the basis of land per AAEU into the upper and lower groups, we find a very substantial difference in other endowments. Livestock wealth is 67 per cent greater per AAEU for the better land-endowed half of all households. Labour force per AAEU is 24 per cent greater and days worked per AAEU are 35 per cent greater. The propensity to own a business is 72 per cent greater. Only the mean educational attainment of the labour force is lower, being 17 per cent below that of the less well-endowed half of all households. It is possible that this is due to the latter group including a few well-educated non-farm households.

Stratifying households on the basis of livestock wealth we consider three groups: those with no livestock, and those with livestock split into upper and lower halves on the basis of livestock wealth per AAEU. Livestock wealth does not appear to be closely associated with other endowments. The high livestock group has 21 per cent more land per AAEU than the low livestock group, but only 87 per cent of the education and 64 per cent of the business ownership of the latter group. Those without livestock tend to occupy an intermediate position between the other groups.

Stratifying by labour force per AAEU we find sharp differences. The group with more labour has 41 per cent more land, 24 per cent more livestock and 92 per cent more business ownership. Stratifying by business ownership reveals no significant differences between those who own and those who do not own businesses for any of the other endowments.

Finally, stratifying by education, households are categorized into three groups: those in which none of the labour force has any education (126 households), and others, who are divided into a high- and a low-education group. Here there are very large differences between groups. The group with no education has 235 per cent more livestock than the group with most education and 124 per cent more than the group with little education. Land ownership displays the same hierarchy, with the uneducated having 21 per cent more land than the most educated and 4 per cent more than those with little education.

To conclude, there is evidence for some degree of endowment concentration between land, livestock, and labour. A household with an atypically large amount of one is likely to have atypically large amounts of the others. Education, however, is negatively related to these endowments and is therefore offsetting.

Predicted income inequalities

We now come to the question of whether the observed differences in endowments between the poor and the non-poor can account for the observed differences in income.

Consider, first, income from crops, which is the single most important component of the difference in total income. Supposing that the poor and the non-poor were operating on the same production function, we should 'explain' the differences in gross crop income per household by entering into the previously estimated crop output production function—the mean value of land, labour on own-shamba, inputs, and the education of the head—for the two groups. Dividing by the number of AAEUs in each group (3.38 for the poor, 3.55 for the non-poor) will yield predicted gross crop income per AAEU for each group. The results are set out in Table 4.12. Of the actual difference in gross crop income per AAEU of 677 shillings, the differences in the four endowments explain 425 shillings, that is, 63 per cent of the total. The remaining 37 per cent is accounted for by the poor achieving a lower return on their endowments than the non-poor. This lower return should not be surprising, for it was predicted by our analysis of differences in

Table 4.12: Predicted and actual gross crop incomes by income class

Endowment	Mean value for		Production function coefficient
	Poor	Non-poor	
Education (level)	2.20	2.56	0.074
Inputs (sh.)	156	279	0.004
Land (acres)	4.73	5.92	0.65
Labour (days)	345	373	0.08
Predicted gross crop income	1 666	3 259	
AAEU	3.38	3.35	
Predicted per AAEU	493	918	
Actual	328	1 005	

cropping patterns. The poor grow disproportionate amounts of low-value food crops on their acreage. In turn this was to some extent explained by overall differences in income: the poor apparently grow a lower relative acreage of cash crops because at very low incomes they can not afford either to finance food purchases or required inputs, or to risk crop failure.

So, 63 per cent of the lower crop income of the poor can be explained directly in terms of their lower endowments, while some of the lower returns on endowments (which account for the remaining 37 per cent) can be explained in terms of overall income differences. Since overall income differences are related to endowment differences, the latter offers a reasonably complete explanation of why the poor receive a lower income from crops than the non-poor. Finally we should note that since the crop income data can be explained by the endowments data, the data obtained from the questionnaires are likely to be substantial. For, were the data insubstantial, income differences would be random with respect to endowments.

We now turn from crop production to livestock income. Our previously estimated livestock income function found that such income depends primarily upon the value of livestock owned. In fact, differences in livestock ownership fully account for differences in livestock income between the poor and the non-poor. We may recall from Table 4.2 that the non-poor had a mean net income from livestock 6.9 times greater (per AAEU) than that of the poor. From Table 4.12 we find that, valued at mean market prices, the non-poor owned 7.3 times as much livestock as the poor. It is apparent that the poor actually succeeded in getting a slightly higher rate of return from their livestock than the non-poor. However, the difference in rates of return is too small to have any statistical reliability and the safest conclusion is that there is no significant difference in rates of return on livestock between the poor and the non-poor. Even this result is quite surprising, for the composition of livestock owned by the poor is very different from that owned by the non-poor. For example, the non-poor own 13 times as many oxen but only 1.1 times as many chickens. This follows from the indivisibility of certain types of livestock, since the more valuable types of livestock can not be owned by those who have only a modest total value of livestock. Indeed, we might expect even those poor households whose total livestock valuation exceeded the unit cost of a valuable animal, to prefer to own many small units of livestock rather than risk one large one: thirty chickens are less likely all to die than is one cow. In the rural areas there is effectively no financial market from which the ordinary peasant household can borrow. Only the richer households, then, can acquire high-value animals. We would therefore have expected that the combination of spreading the risks, together with the inability of poor households to finance the more valuable types of cattle, would have produced a higher rate of return upon higher-value livestock than on low-value livestock. For example, we would have expected a higher rate of return on oxen than on chickens. But if this had been the case, the poor would have had a lower rate of return on their livestock than the non-poor—which they do not. Although with crop income it appears that the poor find it difficult to access the higher-yielding components of the activity—their low income due to lack of endowments being compounded by a lower rate of return on such endowments as they have—in the case of livestock, income differences are entirely explained by differences in the ownership of endowments.

The next component of income to be considered is earned non-farm income. We may remember that there is a very large difference between the mean for the poor (34 shillings per AAEU) and that for the non-poor (503 shillings). This difference cannot be explained by observed differences in endowments. The non-poor have double the propensity to be engaged in some non-farm income earning activity, but even among those so engaged the non-poor earn 7.4 times as much (per AAEU) as do the poor. Our previous attempt to fit an earnings function to the 239 cases of such earnings succeeded only in explaining earning differences in terms of education. Applying the coefficients from this earnings function to the respective endowments of the poor and the non-poor earning non-farm income yields a predicted income differential of only 20 per cent. Having accounted for identified differences in endowments among those working in non-farm activities, the non-poor still earn six times as much as the poor. A small part of this differential is accounted for by differences in the mean number of days worked. Among those engaged in the activities, the poor work for 60 days (per AAEU) and the non-poor for 71 days. This leaves an unexplained differential in earnings per day worked of around 5:1. In part, this is accounted for by the different types of non-farm activity in which the two groups are engaged. The non-poor work 20 per cent more days in non-shamba activities than the poor, they work 230 per cent more days for wages and consequently fewer days on own-businesses. The difference in access to wage work is even more apparent if we look at main occupations, rather than at days worked. Of the 62 workers who cited an activity other than farming as their main occupation, 16 were occupied in handicrafts or construction which were largely their own businesses. Of the remaining 46 who were working primarily for wages, 87 per cent belonged to non-poor households and only 13 per cent to poor households. By contrast, in handicraft and construction activities, 38 per cent of workers came from poor households.

There is, therefore, within non-shamba work a hierarchy of activities and the further up this hierarchy we consider, the more skewed it is against the poor. We have seen in the logit and the earnings function analyses that both access to wage employment and earnings per day in such employment are dependent upon education and age. Access to wage employment is additionally dependent upon gender, women of a given educational level having a lower probability of being employed than men of the same level. However, this does not appear to have a strong influence on inter-household inequalities. The proportion of female-headed households was only slightly greater among the poor (19 per cent) than among the non-poor (15 per cent). In Table 4.13 we show the educational hierarchy of the labour force aged over 20 years old distinguishing between the poor and the non-poor. The upper levels of the hierarchy of educational attainment are again increasingly skewed against the poor. However, even if the 46 wage jobs were filled strictly in

Table 4.13: Educational hierarchy by income class

Education level	Poor	Non-poor	Differential	All
Government secondary school	0	8		8
Private secondary school	1	0		1
Total secondary	1	8	8 : 1	9
Primary standard 8	9	18	2 : 1	27
Cumulative total	10	26	3 : 1	36
Primary standard 7 (males only)	17	39	2 : 1	56
Cumulative total	27	55	2 : 1	82

accordance with this educational hierarchy, the higher educational attainments of the non-poor would be insufficient to explain the concentration of wage occupations. The poor command 28 per cent of the top 46 positions on the educational hierarchy and only 13 per cent of the wage occupation positions. Therefore, although age and education explain most of the differences in access to wage occupations, the poor nevertheless have access to fewer jobs than their education would suggest. This is not surprising. Presumably, educational attainment is not the only way to gain access to a wage job. Those who get a wage job earn an income from it which may well place them among the non-poor; those who have access to a wage job through non-educational criteria will *ex post facto* not be found among the poor, while some of those with sufficient education who nevertheless fail to gain a wage job will be among the poor. To summarize, the poor had virtually the same total labour endowment as the non-poor. Had wage jobs been equally accessible to poor and non-poor households each group would have held 50 per cent of them. Had only the most educated members of the labour force gained the wage jobs, the poor would have had access to only 28 per cent of them, the remaining 72 per cent being taken by the non-poor. The poor held only 13 per cent of the high-wage jobs, so that this shortfall below 28 per cent is the residual, unexplained by differences in educational endowments. Of the overall difference in high-wage income between the poor and the non-poor, around 60 per cent—(50 per cent – 28 per cent)/(50 per cent – 13 per cent)—is attributable to educational endowments and 40 per cent is unattributable. The residual will be categorized as a lower return on identified endowments.

We were unable to explain business income by regression analysis. The poor in fact work more on their own businesses per AAEU than do the non-poor, so their lower income per AAEU from business is solely as a result of lower returns per day worked. We cannot give a statistical explanation for this difference in returns. It seems plausible, however, to think that the poor are pushed into a wide range of marginal activities, low income self-employment being one example of these.

To summarize our discussion of non-farm income, differences between the poor and the non-poor are very pronounced, the earnings of the non-poor being 14.8 times greater than the poor. Overall, this accounts for 30 per cent of the total income gap between the two groups. Yet we have not been able to give a clear explanation of this difference in terms of endowments. We have suggested that around 60 per cent of the differential access to well-paid jobs is accounted for by different educational endowments, but as regards the large differential in earnings per job (7.4 : 1), around 97 per cent could not be explained in terms of education. If we had observed a wider range of worker characteristics, then perhaps earnings would have been more closely related to endowments. Alternatively, the differences in local labour market conditions, or random opportunities, may be the root cause of such large earnings differences. Applying the above figures we assign approximately 60 per cent to account for differential access to education and 3 per cent to account for differential in earnings given access to education. Combined, these account for 11 per cent of the non-farm earnings differential per AAEU, leaving 89 per cent as a residual due to differential returns on endowments. However, these figures are highly tentative.

The final component of income to be considered is that from remittances. Less than 3 per cent of poor households received income from remittances as opposed to 14 per cent of non-poor households. How much a household earns from remittances is determined by the propensity of its members to migrate and the propensity of its migrant members to remit. It is not possible to study either of these propensities very accurately because migrants are by definition absent from villages and so information on their behaviour can only be drawn from a third party. It is known, however, from previous studies that migration in Tanzania is strongly influenced by educational level.[6] It seems likely therefore that, since remittences accrue to households with migrants, remittance income can be related to the educational endowments of households. However, differences in remittance income account for only 5 per cent of the total income gap between the poor and the non-poor. We have no basis for dividing this between endowments and other factors and do not attempt to do so, but fortunately this omission is not substantial.

In our analysis of the origins of poverty we have identified large differences in various income components and have related these differences in varying degrees to differences in endowments. The analysis is summarized in Table 4.14. A little over half of the total income gap between the poor and the non-poor has been traced back to differences in endowments. Among these is the inequality in the

Table 4.14: *Causes of inequality*[a]

Income components of inequality	Total	Due to price differences	Due to cost differences	Due to quantity differences		
				Total remaining	of which due to differences in endowments	of which due to differences in returns on endowments
Subsistence crop	26	0	0	26	27	16
Net crop sales	18	1	0	17	21	0
Livestock income	21	0	0	21	n.a.	n.a.
Remittances	5	n.a.[b]	n.a.	5	4	26
Non-farm income	30	n.a.	n.a.	30		
Total	100	1	0	99	52	42

[a] All figures given as percentages.

[b] n.a. = not applicable.

ownership of livestock which alone accounts for 21 per cent of the total income gap. Other assets of some importance in explaining inequality were education and, to a lesser extent, land. If access to wage employment is regarded as an asset, then it is more significant contributor to inequality than is the concentration in landholdings. Much of the residual inequality may well be indirectly related to endowments. For example, we have suggested that the poor devote less land to cash crops partly because they are short of the assets needed to finance planting them.

The overall picture which emerges is that the poor are poor because of low returns to labour rather than because of labour shortage. These low returns to labour can in turn be explained by the low endowments of non-labour assets owned by the poor. The poor are poor not because they use their endowments less effectively than the non-poor, but because they have fewer endowments to use. This, of course, is significant for equity and poverty alleviation policies, for resource redistribution within rural areas would appear to be capable of reducing the incidence of poverty without reducing output. We return to the policy implications of our analysis of inequality in Chapter 6.

Notes

1. A. Deaton, 'Inequality and needs', *Living Standards Measurement Survey* (Washington DC, World Bank, 1980).
2. Ibid., Households table 2, category 2.
3. A worked example of the conversion from a particular household composition to the measurement of AAEU is set out below:

An example of the estimation of adjusted adult equivalent units (AAEU) from household composition

Household composition	AAEU
Man aged 35	1.00
Woman aged 30	0.88
Woman aged 65	0.72
Boy aged 15	1.20
Boy aged 8	0.64
Girl aged 4	0.48
Girl aged 1	0.40
Household measured in adult equivalent units	5.32
Average cost per adult for household of five adults	0.81
Household measured in Adjusted Adult Equivalent Units	4.29
	$(= 5.32 \times 0.81)$

4. It will be recalled that the Theil Index is defined as:

$$\sum_{i=1}^{n} x_i \log n \, x_i,$$ where x_i is the share of income going to person i.

5. M. E. Lockheed, D. T. Jameson, and J. L. Lau, 'Farmer education and farm efficiency: A survey', *Economic Development and Cultural Change*, 29, 1980.

6. H. N. Barnum and R. H. Sabot, 'Education, employment probabilities, and rural–urban migration in Tanzania', *Oxford Bulletin of Economics and Statistics*, 39, 1977; and P. Collier, 'Migration and unemployment: A dymamic general equilibrium analysis applied to Tanzania', *Oxford Economic Papers*, 31, 1979.

5

The Village Community

Until the 1970s very few Tanzanian peasants lived in villages. The creation of villages has been the principal instrument of Tanzanian rural development policy. Villagization, as we saw in Chapter 3, has not much altered the land endowments of individual households. The benefits of villagization are to be sought, therefore, not in the productive potential of individual households but in a range of communal undertakings. These undertakings can be divided into the social and participatory, and the directly productive. Villages have provided the opportunity for greatly improved provision of social services and active participation by peasants in decision-making. They have also been adopted as the unit for communally owned and operated enterprises. Predominant among these has been the communal shamba which has been touched upon in previous chapters.

We begin our village-level analysis with the provision of social services and participation, which have been the major achievements of villagization.

Facilities and participation

The mean population of the 20 villages in our sample was around 2,500. This is above the average for all officially registered villages, which is around 1,750. The official figures also include some very small registered units. Since the majority of people live in villages of above average size, our sample probably represents the size of village typically inhabited by the rural population. Six villages had populations less than 1,000, the smallest having 320.

Ten of the 20 villages had been established since the Arusha Declaration in 1967. Operation Sogeza (1974), which was the motive force behind settling the rural population in villages, had in our sample generally taken the role of expanding an existing settlement. Only one village had no pre-Sogeza settlement and four villages were relocated as a result of Operation Sogeza. However, ten of the villages which existed prior to Sogeza had had fewer than 100 households each, while by 1980 only one village remained in that size category. In 18 of the villages, the population was reportedly still growing. In 14 villages, some households had recently left the village to settle elsewhere. Nationally, some 300 villages are being established each year, and this resettlement may result in the formation of new villages.

Table 5.1 summarizes a variety of village facilities. Because our sample consisted of only 20 villages, these data cannot be interpreted as being a reliable indicator of facilities generally available in

Table 5.1: Village facilities

	per cent of villages with facility
Social services	
Primary school	100
Secondary school	5
Piped water	60
Clinic	40
Police post	10
Communications	
Regular bus service	55
Market place	50
Crop-buying post	90
Post Office	25
Telephone	10
Participation	
CCM branch	95
CCM youth	80
UWT	85
TAPA	75
Church/mosque	95
Sports club	80
Bar	80
Skills	
Local brick-making	45
Mechanic	20
Carpenter	90
Tailor	85
Baker	25
Butcher	55
Maize grinding	60

Tanzanian villages. The small sample size is compounded by the fact that, although some villages in our sample were remote, survey logistics dictated that villages in the same sample were atypically accessible. Thus, the communications facilities, in particular, were likely to be better than average. Table 5.1 suggests that in the sampled villages social services were well provided. Primary education, health care, and piped water were widely available, thanks to a major national effort. Accommodation was generally provided for secondary school pupils, so that although only one village had a secondary school, all villages had access to secondary schooling. Few children, however, were able to gain places in secondary schools. In the previous year, only around 3 per cent of those village children of an age to enter secondary school actually gained places at government schools. In six of the 20 villages not a single child passed for secondary school.

In addition to social facilities, the government provided an agricultural extension service. Rather than visiting individual farmers the effort of extension work was aimed at the village. The villages in our sample had widely differing access to extension. One village had not been visited by any extension worker in the past year. Two other villages had had visits from a range of extension services with frequent meetings and demonstrations lasting a full day. In our household sample, about a quarter of the households had recently attended a meeting with a *bwana shamba*, as the extension workers are called.

We now turn to the important issue of the distribution of facilities among the rural population. There are some publicly provided facilities from which households benefit in proportion to their income. For example, the extent of benefit from the crop-buying posts provided depends on the amount of crops sold by a particular household. The major social facilities of health and education need not be distributed in such a way. Unfortunately, some studies have shown that in some developing countries even these items of public expenditure disproportionately benefit the wealthier members of the community.[1] We tested whether this was the case in our sample.

First, with regard to health facilities we investigated whether a household's utilization of health clinics was correlated with its income. As a proxy for utilization we adopted the number of vaccinations per child under 5 years of age. This was regressed upon the age of the child and income of the household per AAEU. The coefficient on income was insignificant and negligible. Adding in village dummy variables did not change this result. This is an encouraging finding. It suggests that neither among the whole sample nor within villages is household income a factor which influences use of health facilities. Of course, it could be argued that lower income households have worse health and so ought to make greater use of health services than better-off households. This we also investigated by constructing an indicator of health for children under five. Since enumerators were not medically qualified, the construction of this indicator had to rely upon the Monthly Health Card (MHC) chart combined with parental assessment of child health. If the growth curve on the MHC chart had ever fallen into the red zone, the child was given four points on a sickness index. If, during the past month the child had suffered from diarrhoea, a serious cough or cold, or malaria, then one point was counted for each illness. Thus, an indicator from 0 to 7 was constructed in which the higher the score the worse the health of the child. There was found to be no correlation between this index and income per AAEU. It is possible that this is because of the deficiencies of the index. However, as the results stand they suggest that the problem of ill health, at least among children, is distinct from income levels and distribution.

The analysis was also extended to education. The number of years of primary education for all children aged 7–13 years was regressed upon age and income per AAEU. The results are shown below:

$$E = -3.40^a + 0.49A^a + 0.000095Y^b$$
$$(-15.1) \quad (22.4) \quad (2.2)$$

n = 729
$r^2 = 0.41$
F = 251.7
E = years of primary education
A = age
Y = income per AAEU (in shillings).
^{a} = significant at 1 per cent level
^{b} = significant at 5 per cent level

The results show that there is a weak, but significant, tendency for higher income households to acquire more primary education for their children. An extra 1,000 shillings of income raises the amount of such education by about 1 month, or 6 per cent of the mean amount of education of children in the sample. This suggests that the movement towards universal primary education (UPE) has been distributionally progressive, in an attempt to abolish an otherwise disequalizing tendency of education provision. As very few children were attending secondary school, it was not possible to deduce whether children going to secondary school tended to be from households with above average income.

Finally, we repeated the analysis for access to extension services. Dividing households into those which had recently had contact with the *bwana shamba* and those which had not, the former had incomes per AAEU some 21 per cent higher than the latter—a statistically significant difference at the 5 per cent level. The finding that this publicly-provided facility is regressively distributed is open to several interpretations. It could be that the extension advice has itself caused the income difference, but it is more likely that richer farmers have more time, are less averse to taking risks, and have more to gain from taking extension advice. Either way, as presently distributed, if the extension advice succeeds in raising output it will also, in the process, tend to increase rural inequality.

We now turn to participation in political decision-taking. From Table 5.1 it was evident that the political infrastructure of branches of various party organizations was very widespread. The basic structure for political participation by the rural population had clearly been established.

In addition to the party branches, each village had a structure of committees focusing on finance, crop production, transport, education, and defence. In nearly all cases the committee had met within the past 3 months. The composition of the committees was heavily biased against women, as is shown in Table 5.2. It is particularly

Table 5.2: Composition of village committees

Committee	% women	% villages with no woman member
Finance	11	55
Crop production	11	60
Transport	7	70
Education	29	30
Defence	7	65

striking that on the Crop Production Committee on average only 11 per cent of the members are female, and most villages have no woman member at all. Yet in Tanzania most of the work of growing food is done by women. In our sample, women worked 37 per cent more days than men on household shambas and 15 per cent more days on communal shambas.

Since women are clearly disadvantaged by not being able to participate fully, it is important to discover whether poor households are similarly disadvantaged. Some commentators have suggested that within the villages political power lies with an economic élite of kulaks.[2]

We were to some extent able to test this hypothesis. Households in the sample were asked whether any member of the household was either a ten-cell leader or on the village council. The mean income per AAEU of households with such members was 9 per cent higher than the mean income of households without, though this difference is not statistically significant at the 5 per cent level. Although we cannot distinguish between the influential and the less influential ten-cell leaders, our data suggest that there is no powerful link between wealth and political participation and influence in rural Tanzania. Since, historically, there can be little doubt that there used to be such a link—based on the co-operative societies[3]—the implication is that there has been a shift in power away from the commercially more successful farmers. If this has indeed occurred, then it is a major political achievement.

There appears to remain some problem in encouraging the political participation of the poorer households. Households in which someone was a member of the CCM Party (Chama Cha Mapunduzi or The Party of Change) had an average income per AAEU 25 per cent above those households without CCM membership. Households which had recently attended a CCM meeting had incomes 20 per cent above those which had not. Households which attended the village assembly had incomes 43 per cent above those which did not. Finally, households which attended co-operative meetings had incomes 20 per cent above those which did not. All of these differences are statistically significant at the 5 per cent level.

Effective mobilization of the rural population also requires a good liaison between the villages and the Government. One important way to establish this liaison is for government officials to visit villages. The survey inquired which of 18 categories of officials had visited the village in the last year, examples being the District Development Director and the Tanzania Rural Development Bank (TRDB) representative. The results reveal a high but uneven level of contact. The average village had visits during the year from ten of the eighteen categories of official. Two of the villages were visited by all eighteen categories, while two other villages had only a single visit. This suggests that some villages are on the periphery of official activity, while others receive more attention.

The village economy

In Chapters 3 and 4 we analysed the village economy by considering the economic activities of individual households. Now we introduce two aspects of the village economy which are not fully apparent at the level of the individual household. These are the restricted availability of goods and services and the extent and nature of communal activities. Both are of central importance to the understanding of the village economy.

Limitations on availability of goods and services are of three types: some skills are absent, some agricultural inputs cannot be obtained when they are needed, and some basic consumer goods can only be purchased on an irregular basis. The limited range of skills may be deduced from the heavy preponderance of shamba work and government employment in the employment activities of workers in our sample of households. Table 5.1 reveals that in many villages several important skills are not available. In all 20 villages—for a combined population of some 50,000—there are, for example, only four resident mechanics. This indicates the urgent need to provide training for the rural population. At present the shortage of skills is probably exacerbated by the tendency for trained labour to migrate to the towns.

In addition, agricultural inputs are often scarce and this may be a severe constraint upon output. Farmers were asked whether in the last season seeds, pesticides, and fertilizer had been available when farmers had needed them. For 29 per cent of farmers seeds had not been available, for 63 per cent pesticides had not been available, and for 54 per cent fertilizer had not been available. As might be expected, the main differences were between, rather than within, villages. In six of the villages, almost all farmers had good access to all three items, while in three other villages virtually no farmer was able to obtain any of the three items when they were needed.

As regards the availability of basic consumer goods, the survey investigated whether various items could be bought from shops in the villages. Twenty-one items were considered, including salt, matches, cooking oil, *sembe* (maize flour), *pangas* (sharp knives used for agricultural purposes), and cigarettes. None of the twenty-one items was available in every village; on average, only thirteen of them were available. There were marked differences between villages: in one village all twenty-one items were available while in five other villages only eight items or fewer were available. The widespread chronic shortage of basic goods may well have serious repercussions on agricultural output, for if peasants cannot buy goods they may choose not to sell food or other crops. If they choose not to sell crops they may choose not to grow them, and if a surplus of crops is not available for export this will contribute to loss of foreign exchange. The attendant macro-economic problems will be discussed briefly in Chapter 6.

We now turn to the second major feature of the village economy, namely communal activities.

The communal economy

It is already clear from Chapter 3 that the communal economy plays a major part in the lives of most village households. Around 20 per cent of total labour time is spent on the communal shamba and around a further 5 per cent on communal non-farm activities.[4] The extent of communal activities varies considerably between villages. While two villages had no communal shamba, several operated very large holdings. On average 8 per cent of cultivated land was farmed communally. The survey also attempted to gather data on the quantity and value of communal output over the preceding four years. Unfortunately, records in some villages were poor and the resulting data unreliable. The average value of output from the communal shamba was around 9,500 shillings in the most recent year. While this is a useful income for the village it is small in relation to the resources devoted to the communal shamba. The output per household from the village communal farm is only some 28 shillings in comparison with an average of 2,160 shillings from individual plots. The communal shamba absorbs approximately 20 per cent of village labour and 8 per cent of village land, yet it produces less than 2 per cent of agricultural output, according to our sample. Although this might be unusual (or due to errors of measurement), it is in broad conformity with a recent government survey of communal production in over 4,000 villages. Returns per acre were found to be very low, the average value of output from the communal shamba being around 25,000 shillings.

Several aspects of the communal shamba give cause for concern. First, we may recall from Chapter 4 that work on the communal shamba is done disproportionately by the poorer half of the community. It is therefore an example of regressive taxation. It would be more equitable to tax income, livestock, or land than to tax labour, which is the main endowment of the poor. This is then compounded by the fact that the poor contribute more of their labour than do the wealthy, and so, in effect, pay a higher rate of tax.

The problem of poor distribution of contributions to the communal economy coexists with the problem of low productivity. On the communal shamba output per acre, and particularly output per worker, appears to be considerably below that on individual shambas. The low output per worker in communal agriculture is serious, for there is no evidence to suggest a labour surplus and the output of most households is probably labour-constrained. The present organization of the communal shambas thus appears to involve a substantial diversion of around 20 per cent of village labour into activities of very low productivity. Such a diversion is lowering income levels, especially of the rural poor, without generating much village revenue.

It is therefore very important to discover why the communal shamba is currently so unproductive. Our data suggest two reasons. First, there appears to be a substantial mismatch between land and labour. The communal shamba is allocated over twice as much labour per acre as the individual shambas. We may remember that this labour input is even throughout the year and is not related to the seasonal cycle of labour requirements, since the by-laws typically require each household to contribute for example two days' labour per week. Since about 80 per cent of communal labour is currently absorbed by the shamba, during much of the year this large labour contribution is probably not needed. Although the communal shamba absorbs more labour per acre than individual shambas the crop mix on the communal shamba is biased away from labour-intensive crops. For example, labour-intensive crops—such as tea and coffee—which are grown on many of the individual shambas, are not cultivated on any of the communal shambas in our sample. In the previous season only six crops had been grown communally and the acreage was heavily dominated by maize and sorghum. Only one village had introduced commercial crops—pyrethrum and sunflower. Although the communal crop mix indicated a lower labour requirement per acre than on individual shambas, in practice labour input was higher. This suggests that rural labour surplus arises on the communal shamba rather than in individual households. Rather than mobilizing labour surplus, present arrangements may even be creating it.

The second reason for low communal productivity seems to be connected with the way in which communal output is used. The Village Survey inquired whether output was distributed to households in proportion to the labour contribution which they had made. As we can see from the Household Survey, very little communal output was distributed to households (either in cash or in kind) on any basis. In fact, only in three villages was there a distribution of communal output linked to household labour contributions. We know that because the poor contribute most of the labour such distributions are progressive. It is interesting that each of these three villages had communal output substantially above average. The mean value of communal output in these three villages was six times greater than the mean value in the remaining villages. This suggests that the effort devoted to work on the communal shamba can be substantially increased by a more widespread use of distributions of output on a basis which has been approved. However, the association between communal output and its distribution is open to an alternative interpretation, namely that if output is high then proportionately more of output is distributed.

The above evidence on the communal shamba indicates that complacency would be inappropriate. As presently operated, the majority of communal shambas cannot be viewed as successful for they are probably causing a net loss of output and worsening income distribution. Only in a few villages does the communal shamba appear to be successful. It is important to learn from the diverse forms of communal experiment which ingredients enable communal systems to succeed so that these can be used more widely. One limitation of the introduction of labour-related distribution systems (if indeed such systems induce higher productivity) is that they require reliable record-keeping in which workers can place their confidence. The widespread absence of records on communal outputs suggests that, despite efforts to train village bookkeepers, many villages still lack the required skills. A recent government survey has suggested that one reason for this is the very high turnover of village bookkeepers, perhaps because—once trained—they tend to seek jobs in towns.

Although the shamba was the major focus for communal activity, several other communal activities were found in most villages. Nine of the villages owned some communal livestock and two had communally owned lorries. Half of the villages had received loans from the Government to finance a variety of projects. Nineteen of the villages had undertaken some self-help project during the period 1976–1980. The most common form of such projects was the establishment and running of a village shop (seventeen villages), followed by building classrooms for the village school (thirteen), and the building of a CCM office (nine). Other service facilities provided on a self-help basis included an improved water system (four villages) and a newly constructed health clinic (two). There were fewer production-oriented projects. Nine villages had a communal maize grinder and in eight there had been some communal road construction. In three villages there was a communal crafts factory and in one a communal soap factory. Poultry is sometimes raised as a communal activity.

Communal activities are strikingly orientated towards agriculture. Only 20 per cent of communal labour time is devoted to other activities and these are mostly non-productive. Communal enterprise is at present not diversifying the village economy; rather it is replicating the existing pattern of activities under another mode of organization. The communal mode may in principle be a means of mobilizing resources, that is, a means of raising public revenue; it may be a means of redistribution; and finally it may facilitate economies of organization not available at the level of the individual household. Unfortunately, it is apparent that in Tanzania agriculture is not a sector in which the potential benefits of the communal mode of production can be readily actualized.

Communal agriculture is directly generating only a small volume of public resources even though nearly all communal output is retained by the village. Indirectly, communal agriculture is causing a loss of potential public resources because of the high opportunity cost of the labour resources used in communal production. Peasant agriculture, we have argued, is largely labour-constrained. According to our survey data, if the labour now going into communal agriculture were diverted into peasant agriculture, labour input into peasant agriculture would increase by 36 per cent. An increase in crop output which approached this magnitude would generate far more public resources than currently achieved through the retention of communal output. This is because the implicit taxation of peasant agricultural output is quite considerable. The principal determinants of this taxation are the official maize price to farmers, which is probably less than half the market-clearing price, and the exchange rate at which peasant foreign exchange earnings are converted into shillings, which now clearly bears no relation to a market-clearing rate. Approximately half of the true value of marketed output accrues to the public authorities in the form of these implicit taxes. Of course, by no means all of peasant crop output is marketed. According to our survey data, around 42 per cent of gross crop output was marketed. This is similar to the estimate made by the Bureau of Statistics in the National Accounts which puts marketed output at 40 per cent of total agricultural output for the same period. We have previously estimated that the communal shamba may be yielding some 2 per cent of peasant crop output to the public authorities. Were the labour used in this activity redeployed on peasant holdings so as to generate only an additional 5 per cent of gross crop output, then public revenue would be unaffected. Of the 5 per cent extra peasant output, around 2 per cent would be marketed. But since about half of the value of marketed output accrues to public revenue, the 2 per cent crop value accruing to peasants is matched by another 2 per cent accruing to public revenue. The above calculation is highly imprecise, for neither communal crop output nor the implicit taxation of crop output, nor for that matter the division of marginal output between subsistence and the market, are known with any accuracy. However, there is room for considerable inaccuracy before communal agriculture can be regarded as anything other than a net drain on public revenue, for the break-even point of 5 per cent extra peasant output must be set against the 36 per cent extra labour that could be devoted to peasant holdings.

Communal agriculture is probably causing a net reduction in public revenue. Of equal importance to this reduction are the distributional consequences of communal agriculture which are highly regressive. As presently constituted, participation in communal agriculture is a tax borne predominantly by the poor. Among poor households 28 per cent of total labour time is devoted to this effectively unremunerated activity as compared with only 20 per cent of labour time devoted by non-poor households. Communal agriculture is therefore apparently having an adverse effect on income distribution. The above figures understate the extent to which the system is regressive because contributions amount to a labour tax, and labour is the one asset which poor and non-poor households possess in equal measure. We will return to this point shortly.

The final possible benefit of communal production comes from economies of organization. In fact, unlike industry, agriculture in Tanzania is not usually characterized by economies of scale. The present concentration of communal activities upon agriculture, therefore, may be misplaced. Furthermore, by contrast with industrial jobs, agricultural work is diverse and can rarely be monitored, and we would therefore expect problems of incentive and enforcement to be more severe. This certainly appears to be the case at present. Clearly, communal agriculture as at present operated in Tanzania is a less efficient mode of organization than individual peasant agriculture.

Taken together with the previous discussion on tax revenue and distribution, this implies a basic contradiction in the present design of communal production, for the twin objectives of resource mobilization and redistribution can not both be achieved by this one policy instrument. If communal production is to mobilize significant resources, that is, raise public revenue, it must remunerate labour contributed to communal activities at less than what labour could earn in peasant agriculture for the communal mode of production is at best no more productive than peasant agriculture. Furthermore, if the Putterman solutions described in Chapter 1—whereby all the output attributable to labour would be distributed to that labour—were to be adopted, the remaining surplus would at best be very small. This is because land for peasant agriculture is abundant whereas there is a very high labour-to-land ratio in communal agriculture. Were communal labour to be rewarded according to its marginal product in peasant agriculture, this would more than exhaust the total output of the communal shamba. Given the difference in land-labour ratios between peasant and communal agriculture, this would remain the case even if efficiency in the communal mode could be improved to the extent that the communal shamba was operating on the same production function as peasant agriculture.

Resource mobilization requires that labour be under-remunerated for communal agricultural work. That is, there must be an implicit tax on labour if communal agriculture is directly to augment public revenue. This is a different point from our earlier argument that indirectly communal agriculture reduces public revenue by reducing peasant marketed output. Recall that in Tanzania such a tax is doubly regressive. Not only is labour the one asset owned by the poor, but they contribute a greater proportion of their labour to the communal shamba than do non-poor households. If the purpose of communal agriculture is to mobilize public resources it will worsen income distribution. Alternatively, if remuneration for labour were raised to a level at which there were no regressive consequences, communal agriculture would not—even directly—generate public revenue. This very serious dilemma has not really been addressed, although there is a casual belief that the communal shamba is increasing total crop output, generating public resources, and improving income distribution all at the same time. The policy dilemma goes deeper than the observation that none of these objectives is currently being achieved: with this particular mode of intervention the objectives are actually contradictory.

None of the above problems need necessarily apply to communal non-agricultural productive enterprises. Labour tasks are more easily monitored and economies of scale are powerful. It would in principle be possible to remunerate labour at a rate above mean earnings in peasant activities and still generate a substantial surplus. Such a level of remuneration would be equalizing because, as we have seen, due to a lack of assets poor households currently achieve much lower returns on their labour than non-poor households. It may be assumed that the labour of poor households would then choose to work on communal activities, while the labour of non-poor households would choose not to do so. Far from being coerced into providing communal labour, the unwillingness of non-poor households to provide communal labour would in such circumstances be welcome, for it would imply more employment opportunities for the labour of poor households. Both poor and non-poor households would benefit, and if the non-poor were required to make some non-labour contributions to the village, public resources would be raised.

The design of non-agricultural communal activities in villages is only now beginning to receive appropriate attention. The ILO has initiated a project, now supported by several other international organizations, to stimulate village-level participation in the design and implementation of such communal undertakings. Given that there are so few rural communal industries currently operating, a variety of pragmatic experimental interventions is likely to be the best way of learning about rural development.

A corollary of the orientation of communal activities towards agriculture and of the failure of those activities to mobilize resources has been that the villages directly provide very few of the social service facilities now available to them. Indirectly, of course, through the high taxation of peasant marketed output, peasants have paid for the substantial improvement in health, education, and water facilities described earlier in the chapter. But because this financing is indirect, the village as an organizational unit currently lacks control over the public facilities located in the village. It is widely recognized as desirable that villages should achieve greater operational control over facilities and a village revenue base is clearly conducive to such control. Because communal agriculture cannot generate such a revenue base without involving unacceptably regressive redistributions of income, and because communal activities other than agriculture will take many years to develop, some other policy initiative appears appropriate. This we discuss in our final chapter.

Interconnections between village characteristics

One of the major themes of Chapter 4 was that the bulk of income inequality and absolute poverty arose from differences within rather than between villages. We may recall that 84 per cent of inequality in household incomes was found to be due to differences within villages. The 50 per cent of villages with the highest incidence of 'poverty' had only 64 per cent of the poor households in the sample.[5] We now explore whether the various village characteristics, other than household income, are correlated with each other or with household income. For example, we have previously identified the fact that in some villages the availability of basic consumer goods was better than in others and we have also established that some villages had much closer contact with government officials than others. We now investigate whether some villages appear to be systematically favoured, whether there are links between participation and the performance of the communal shamba, and whether any of these are linked to differences in the level of household incomes between villages.

Six indicators were constructed in an attempt to summarize various aspects of the villages. As a simple measure of contact with government officials we chose eighteen categories of officials visiting the village over the previous year. This gave a score range from 0 to 18. As an indicator of local participation we chose from the Household Survey the proportion of sampled households in a village which had recently attended the village assembly, a co-operative meeting, or a CCM meeting, or were CCM members. The resulting index ranged from 0 to 100. As an indicator of facilities available in the village we used a check-list of twenty-eight services and facilities which might be available, given an index range from 0 to 28. As an indicator of the availability of basic consumer goods we similarly used a check-list of twenty-one items which might be available in the village shops. Our indicator of the performance of the communal shamba was simply deduced from the value of output. Finally, as an indicator of access to extension advice we combined the Village Survey data on visits and demonstrations by extension staff and the Household Survey data on the proportion of sampled households in a village which had recent contact with the extension service. The indicator ranged from 0 to 20. The six indicators were then correlated with each other and with the mean income per AAEU of sampled households in each village.

The results are set out in Table 5.3. In most instances correlations were found to be low. The most powerful correlation was between the extent of contact with the government officials and the provision of facilities in the village (a correlation significant at the $2\frac{1}{2}$ per cent level). This is open to several interpretations and may indicate that facilities attract officials or that officials are needed to establish facilities. Both are also correlated with the availability of goods. This interconnection between contact with officials, village facilities, and availability of goods is the clearest indication in the data of a 'virtuous circle' syndrome of village characteristics. None of the three,

Table 5.3: Correlation matrix of village indicators

	Mean income	Government contact	Participation	Facilities	Goods availability	Communal shamba	Extension
Mean income	1.00 (0.00)[a]						
Government contact	-0.11 (0.66)	1.00 (0.00)					
Participation	0.29 (0.22)	-0.08 (0.75)	1.00 (0.00)				
Facilities	-0.09 (0.69)	0.50 (0.02)	0.02 (0.95)	1.00 (0.00)			
Goods availability	0.11 (0.66)	0.37 (0.11)	0.35 (0.13)	0.31 (0.18)	1.00 (0.00)		
Communal shamba	0.06 (0.80)	0.26 (0.27)	-0.20 (0.40)	0.12 (0.61)	0.00 (1.00)	1.00 (0.00)	
Extension	0.09 (0.70)	0.15 (0.53)	0.64 (0.00)	0.22 (0.35)	0.26 (0.27)	-0.15 (0.53)	1.00 (0.00)

[a] Terms in parentheses are levels of significance. Number of observations is 20.

however, is correlated with living standards as measured by mean household income per AAEU.

The only other significant correlation is between participation in village political meetings and contact with the extension service. This is not surprising as extension contacts are also through meetings. It appears that in some villages meetings are more successful than in others.

Neither mean income nor the performance of the communal shamba is correlated with any of the other indicators. If the indicators rightly reflect what they are designed to measure, this is important. It suggests that the distinction between high- and low-income villages might not be as important for other village characteristics as has sometimes been suggested. Furthermore, it suggests that successful communal activities might depend less upon the extent of participation in the village political process and the level of economic development than upon the particular basis of operation of the communal activity itself.

Since our indicators of village characteristics are highly imperfect, our conclusion from the above analysis—that villages generally do not fit easily onto a unidimensional spectrum of success—can only be tentative. If this is correct, then it further strengthens the findings of Chapter 4 that the major disequalizing factors are to be found within villages rather than stemming from any differences between villages. This has powerful implications for policy design.

Notes

1. J. Meerman, *Public Expenditure in Malaysia: Who Benefits and Why?* (New York, Oxford University Press, 1979).
2. M. von Freyhold, *Ujamaa Villages in Tanzania: Analysis of a Social Experiment* (London, Heinemann, 1979).
3. J. Iliffe, *A Modern History of Tanganyika* (Cambridge, Cambridge University Press, 1979) and R. C. Pratt, *The Critical Phase in Tanzania, 1945–68, Nyerere and the Emergence of a Socialist Strategy*, African Studies Series, No. 25 (Cambridge, Cambridge University Press, 1976).
4. From Table 3.8, 23.6 per cent of days worked are spent on the communal shamba; in terms of hours per week the total is 7.1 hours per worker. Depending upon assumptions about the length of the typical working week, the share of communal shamba time in total hours worked lies in the range of 15 per cent to 21 per cent. The ratio of communal non-farm work to shamba work was 1 : 4 (Table 3.11). As part of the Village Ques-

tionnaire we asked the number of able adults in the village, the number who worked on the communal shamba, and the number of days per week typically worked on the communal shamba by this group. Assuming a six-day working week, the share of total days worked on the communal shamba thus averaged 22.5 per cent: this was very close to the 23.6 per cent derived from the Household Questionnaire.

5. That is, those households in the poorer half of the sample population.

6

Poverty, Labour, and Rural Development Policy

Because of the importance of agriculture in our development, one would expect that agriculture and the needs of the agricultural producers would be the beginning, and the central reference point, of all our economic planning. Instead, we have treated agriculture as if it was something peripheral, or just another activity in the country, to be treated on a par with all the others, and used by the others without having any special claim upon them ... We are neglecting agriculture .... We must now stop this neglect of agriculture. We must now give it the central place in all our development planning. For agriculture is indeed the foundation of all our progress.

Julius K. Nyerere (20 October 1982)

Rural development in Tanzania: lessons of experience

Almost two decades have elapsed since the Arusha Declaration which promised 'self-reliant development' in Tanzania. Since then a substantial transformation has taken place especially in the rural areas, but the results have not always been what was originally desired. At present Tanzania is an example of the deepening crisis of Africa. An elaborate institutional structure has been created which is based on the Villagization Programme. This structure was designed to promote growth and achieve equity, but experience suggests that these objectives have not been attained. An acute balance-of-payments problem has conditioned the performance of the economy and lack of foreign exchange has led to a reduction of essential imports. Industry runs at a very low capacity (20 to 30 per cent), the programme of social services is subject to severe constraints, and public expenditure has been curtailed. The need for external resources has led to questions being raised about the viability of the Tanzanian political and economic model. For instance, the International Monetary Fund and the World Bank have asked for important structural changes, especially in the areas of increasing incentives for agriculture producers and the devaluation of the currency to promote exports. The Tanzania Government has counteracted this by introducing its own programme of structural adjustment which aims to reform the economy without sacrificing the existing distributional policies.

It is against this background that the present study was carried out. Its main objective was to generate a set of data for understanding and assessing the performance of the agrarian economy of Tanzania. Previously the various written works on Tanzania had suffered from the lack of such a data base. Moreover, the evaluative part of the study provides a backdrop to the present agrarian crisis. It is hoped that this approach to the Tanzanian experience can also be instructive for other African economies.

The lessons analysed in the three preceding chapters may be summarized under three broad headings: the nature of the agrarian economy, the extent of rural inequality, and the role of institutional innovation—especially that of communal production.

Taken as a whole, Tanzania possesses a very thin, undiversified rural economy. Subsistence production remains a large share of total activity, there is only a narrow range of skills available, and employment is dominated by peasant crop production. There are few non-labour assets and hardly any people are educated beyond the primary level. Those who do gain secondary education migrate to the towns from where few choose to return. Rural isolation is compounded by a poor transport system and limited availability of even the most basic goods. In this way, Tanzania's economy is in sharp contrast with many other peasant economies which are characterized by a dense network of market transactions and a wide variety of economic activities. Although Tanzania's rural economy is sparse, it is nevertheless differentiated, and there is a considerable amount of inequality between peasant households. Income concentration in peasant economies is sometimes associated with commercialization; rural Tanzania, on the other hand, combines an uncommercialized economy with considerable inequality. Finally, as discussed in Chapter 5, villages have succeeded as organizational units for the provision of public services but have not yet succeeded as organizational units for public production. In developing these themes, we begin by discussing the series of unresolved issues raised at the beginning of this book.

We may recall from Chapter 1 that the first issue raised was concerned with the extent of rural inequality: was it indeed the case that 'all peasants look alike'? Unambiguously, this issue can be resolved in the negative. With a Theil index of inequality of 0.40 and the income data corroborated by being related to endowments, rural differentiation is a fact. This becomes more surprising when it is related to our second hypothesis, that most inequality arises within villages. We began by questioning whether the inequalities are predominantly ecological, and therefore identifiable as differences between villages, or predominantly socio-economic, and therefore identifiable as differences within the villages? Our selected villages were highly diverse (see Table 2.1). They included highlands, plains, and coasts, and a range of rainfall from 400 mm. to 2,000 mm. per annum. Neighbourhood population density ranged from very low to very high, and land availability from plentiful to scarce. Cattle ownership ranged from nil to high, and communications ranged from good—with a nearby regional headquarters—to very poor—with no urban influence. In short, the selected villages reflect, at least approximately, the diversity of Tanzania's 8,000 villages. We emphasize this because we found that despite such wide ecological variety only 16 per cent of overall inequality could be explained by inter-village differences. In other words, 84 per cent of inequality resulted from intra-village differences.

We suggested that, if inter-village inequality was important, then centralized control of rural development would be necessary for greater egalitarianism. Since inequality between villages is unimportant there is a strong case for decentralized authority. However, centralized authority might still be necessary if political power within villages resides with economic élites. However, evidence did not substantiate this. The households of councillors and ten-cell leaders did not have incomes significantly higher than those of other households, and although membership of the CCM and attendance at political meetings were associated with significantly higher household income, the magnitude of the income differences was small when compared with overall inequalities. Therefore, neither of the potential objections to the decentralization of power to the village level does in fact hold.

Other hypotheses raised in Chapter 1 focused upon the possible trade-off between equity and efficiency. We found that in agriculture there was little difference between poor and non-poor households as regards the returns on non-labour resources: the poor were poor not because they misused their resources but because they had so few non-labour resources. This suggests that a policy of redistribution of non-labour resources could increase equity without reducing efficiency. The most commonly deployed policy of this type is that of land reform, which has apparently been implemented in Tanzania. However, we found that Operation Sogeza had reduced the mean acreage cultivated rather than altering land concentration, and it should therefore be regarded neither as a land reform nor as a failed attempt at such. Moreover, we found that land reform would in any case have been inappropriate in Tanzania since the poor did not own substantially less land than the non-poor.

In Chapter 1 the provision of social services raised three issues: inequality of access, whether some villages were systematically favoured, and whether there were any productive benefits from social expenditures. In Chapter 5 we found that access to health and education services was largely unrelated to income. There was some tendency for villages which had good facilities also to have close contacts with government officials and better availability of goods, but these interconnections were weak and could partly be explained by differences in village locations and size. Taken together, these findings suggest that the provision of social facilities has not only increased enormously (as is well documented) but that this provision is equitably distributed. It is difficult to measure the productive benefits of public expenditure and we attempted to do so only in the case of education. While education made a substantial contribution to wage earnings, this relationship is open to several interpretations, not all of which afford a socially productive role to education. The performance of education in the crop production function was encouraging, and household heads who had completed primary education, we estimated, raised the value of crop output decisively—by around 25 per cent—compared with illiterate household heads. Since, from Table 3.3, the majority of senior adults had at most only attended literacy classes, most of the output gains from past investments in education have still to come into effect, as those who are currently being educated form households and become agricultural decision-takers. Since at present virtually no secondary school leavers become farmers, we are unable to estimate the potential productive benefits of education beyond the primary level.

The remaining hypotheses raised in Chapter 1 relate to communal production, namely whether performance was related to the structure of incentives or to village characteristics, and whether communal production could be regarded as harnessing surplus labour, thus having an opportunity cost only in leisure. We found a distinct relationship between the incentive system and performance. Where workers were remunerated in relation to their work—and much output was distributed on this basis—communal output was substantially higher. There was no evidence relating the performance of the communal shamba to village circumstances, such as the level of participation in decisions, or mean household income. This suggests that improvements in the performance of the communal shamba neither require nor can be induced by general village-level interventions, but can be achieved by altering the incentive system. The labour allocation data in Chapter 3 suggested that communal activities would have a substantial opportunity cost in terms of other output since surplus labour was not widespread. In fact, as a policy instrument, the communal shamba appeared to worsen income distribution, reducing public revenue and total agricultural output. It is, therefore, flawed in that it is moving society away from the three policy goals which it is intended to achieve.

It is important to emphasize this distinction between policy instruments and policy goals since instruments, once implemented, become part of the status quo and are therefore liable to become emotively confused with objectives. For communal crop production to be treated as a goal in itself is to argue that irrespective of its consequence for inequality, living standards, food supply, and revenue, it is desirable. This was probably not what induced policy-makers and advisers to implement Ujamaa, but rather a belief that this was a means of attaining equitable growth as, indeed, communal agriculture has been in China, although with radically different conditions and modes of organization.[1]

The problem which policy-makers perceived was that the commercialization of peasant agriculture would benefit primarily a minority of prosperous peasants who would develop into a kulak class, thereby generating substantial inequality. The chosen policies were to turn the terms of trade against peasants, reduce market networks, regulate landholdings, introduce communal production, and provide basic social services. Collectively, all but the last have tended to reduce agricultural production and incomes while a fairly high degree of rural inequality has persisted. The current crisis in

Tanzanian agriculture, together with the joint inadequacy of marketed food production and of foreign exchange to generate production, has led policy-makers to reappraise the situation. Their reappraisal is enunciated in a new policy statement which represents a remarkable reversal for it encourages private, foreign, and large-scale enterprises to establish large farms.[2] Their willingness to rely upon foreign capital and large-scale private commerce, and consequently to accept the emergence of a landless, wage-earning rural proletariat, shows that they are prepared to abandon cherished concepts. This shift in policy from faith in communal agriculture to faith in commercial farms has 'overshot' the option of encouraging a commercial peasantry—presumably owing to the persistent fear of kulaks. Yet our survey evidence suggests that this fear is misplaced, and that the new solution of large-scale commercial farms is likely to be little more successful than the experiment in communal agriculture. These are broad statements which we now substantiate.

What is a kulak? Clearly, if a kulak were merely a prosperous peasant, then there would be an irreconcilable contradiction involved in attempting to raise rural living standards through developing peasant activities while trying to prevent the emergence of kulaks. However, what is implied by the term is rather a type of household which cultivates substantially more land than could be done by means of its own labour, by hiring labour from a dependent group of landless or near-landless households. Defined in this way, the number of kulaks in Tanzania is negligible. In our random sample of 600 household, not a single household used significant amounts of hired labour. In a few areas of Tanzania, a few households will approximate to this description, but the numbers are evidently so small that, at present, kulaks need not be considered in policy formulation. The issue is, therefore, whether such a class could emerge so rapidly as to be uncontrollable. In fact, the emegence of kulaks is unlikely for the same reason that they do not exist at present, namely, because land is abundant in Tanzania. It was shown in Chapter 3 that there is no landlessness, so that workers always have the option of working on their own holdings rather than as hired labourers. At present, they invariably choose the former option. In Chapter 4, we showed that production in peasant agriculture was subject to diseconomies of scale. Taken together with the fairly equal distribution of land and the absence of a land market, this implies that as long as households are on similar production functions it will not benefit one household to sell its labour to another rather than work on its own holding.

The proviso of similar production functions is clearly met in Tanzania to the extent that it is related to the agricultural technology employed. Because market access is at present limited and risky, it is quite possible that some households in effect have access to production opportunities denied to other households. In such a situation it could be profitable for the hiring of labour to emerge despite an abundance of land. But this argument suggests that it is the very thinness and unreliability of market networks which generate the potential for a kulak class. Widening market access would probably remove the circumstances under which peasant-generated development would widen inequalities. In fact, in Tanzania's present circumstances, widening market access is likely to be equalizing, since, as shown in Chapter 4, the poor are not poor because of involvement in exploitative economic relationships, but because they have such little participation in markets.

This is not to argue that a commercialized peasantry would automatically produce an egalitarian distribution of income, nor that a policy of improving the terms of trade for peasants would do other than benefit primarily the more prosperous peasants. However, there is no reason to believe that a peasantry with wider access to and participation in market transactions would have a distribution of income any more unequal than the present distribution. At present, although most of the gains from higher prices for marketed crops would accrue to the richer half of the peasantry, inequality would be reduced. Around 75 per cent of the benefits would accrue to the richer 50 per cent of households on unchanged market participation. Before dismissing these benefits it should be recalled that most of these 'richer' households are in absolute terms rather poor. Furthermore, because gross cash crop income is more equally distributed between poor and non-poor households than is total income, an increase in prices for cash crops would tend to equalize relative incomes: the incomes of poor households would rise proportionately more than those of non-poor households. Finally, market participation—if combined with improved market access—would lead to greater market opportunities which would benefit poor households currently denied access.

Benign peasant commercialization has been obstructed on the false premise that commercialization would introduce inequality and would lead to the formation of kulak class. We have suggested that this premise is false in two respects, namely, that commercialization would not produce kulaks and that Tanzanian peasant agriculture already has substantial inequalities. The policy of obstructing peasant commercialization has exacted a price in terms of average peasant living standards without in fact addressing these inequalities. The successful policy of providing social services cannot be extended without improved revenue, yet this appears to be incompatible with improving the peasant terms of trade as this would reduce the implicit taxation of agriculture.

A policy instrument is needed which would raise revenue and yet do so more equitably than either crop taxation or communal labour. On the basis of our analysis of income sources and asset ownership, the appropriate object of taxation appears to be livestock. Livestock income is at present highly unequal, there being a sevenfold differential between poor and non-poor households, and this income differential is entirely accounted for by the different values of livestock owned. As a result, nearly 90 per cent of the revenue from a livestock tax would be paid by the richest 50 per cent of households. If we are right in our claim that power in villages does not rest with an economic élite of livestock owners, then village authorities—if allowed to retain the revenue in the village—would have both the information and the incentive to implement such a tax. The revenue could be used to finance both social facilities and communal non-agricultural enterprises as discussed in Chapter 5. Without doubt, a locally administered livestock tax, like any tax, has many obstacles and disadvantages. However, when compared with either the communal shamba or with crop taxation it appears to be a more efficient method of attaining similar objectives.

Rural development policy in time of crisis

The crisis of the Tanzanian economy, referred to at the outset of this chapter, manifests itself in an acute shortage of foreign exchange, dearth of consumer goods, limited availability and higher relative price of food, fuel shortage, urban un- and underemployment, and a stagnating agrarian economy. One result of the crisis has been the growth of a 'parallel economy'. The country's informal economy has claimed much of the produce of the predominantly peasant agricultural sector.[3] Peasants appear to have shifted from export and non-food crops to food crops for their own subsistence and for local, informal trading.

This crisis has not gone unnoticed by the Tanzanian leadership. As early as 1967, President Nyerere—in his *Essay on Socialism and Rural Development*—recognized the weaknesses of traditional African agriculture and sought to build on indigenous institutions to bring about self-reliant development. Yet the present crisis shows that the institutional policy reforms which were introduced have not constituted sufficient conditions for rural development.

The question of how to face up to this agrarian crisis is fundamental. The answers put forward represent two polarized positions: the World Bank view reflected in the Berg Report[4] and the Sector Survey,[5] and that of the Tanzanian leadership. The Bank starts from the premise that, in Tanzania as well as in other parts of Africa, 'the record is grim and it is no exaggeration to talk of crisis',[6] and it assumes that the causes of institutional failure and peasant disengagement lie in the absence of price incentives at the producers' level. The Tanzanian Government, on the other hand, feels that a sharp increase in the price of agricultural commodities, especially maize, and a massive devaluation of the Tanzanian shilling would not necessarily lead to the desired increase in agricultural productivity and exports.[7] However, it has responded by forming the Task Force on National Agricultural Policy in 1982 and publishing the Agricultural Policy of Tanzania paper (April 1983: hereafter referred to as the 'Policy Paper'). With regard to its rural development strategy, the Government has adopted a compromise, concentrating on maintaining its primary objectives while making significant concessions to the structural adjustment programme proposed by the Bank and the IMF.[8]

The Policy Paper spelt out the main features of a programme which aims to achieve agricultural recovery without sacrificing the present institutional framework. The paper admits the need to adopt a policy approach that responds to the needs of the peasantry rather than idealizing them. Thus, the Policy Paper recognizes the need for 'institutional pluralism' which calls for the coexistence of different forms of ownership: private as well as communal. In this respect the Policy Paper recommends that co-operative unions, which were dissolved in 1976, be restored. This is regarded as a step towards restricting the role of parastatals, since the latter will have to deal with unions rather than with individual villages. The need to motivate peasants to participate in the design and implementation of the development programme has also been stressed. It is hoped that this can be achieved primarily through solving the problem of insecurity of tenure, for the government has speculated that one reason for the neglect of land is the lack of such security. The Paper recognizes that it is 'essential that all users feel confident that their investments of effort and money will be beneficial to them and their families as well as the nation as a whole.'[9] Thus it is recommended that land leases of thirty-three to ninety-nine years should be granted to individual farms.

Moreover, it has been suggested that satellite villages be created to deal with the problem of distance between place of residence and place of work. However, communal farms are still supported on the grounds that they are 'one of the major sources of village government funds'. The broadening of trading options for individual farms is also recommended in order to increase efficiency and encourage exports without abandoning overall public marketing of traded agricultural commodities. National marketing institutions are to leave production and processing responsibilities to the private sector. Villages and the restored co-operative unions will be able to trade with 'adjacent societies'—local retailers for processing—and with public marketing bodies. Finally, reforms of agricultural pricing policy are proposed. These include an attempt to establish more realistic estimates of production costs, favouring foreign exchange-earning crops through increase in relative prices, announcing producer prices in good time before the planting season, and setting consumer prices to encourage the consumption of those foodstuffs which Tanzania is well-suited to produce.[10]

The Policy Paper, by emphasizing the need for decentralization, institutional pluralism, peasant participation, and the liberalization of restrictions on the private sector presents a possible package for the recovery of Tanzanian agriculture. Reform of the agrarian economy is the key to coping with the present crisis. The agricultural sector is in turn dependent upon the performance of the rest of the economy, in particular for the supply of inputs and consumer goods. This interdependence of the micro-economic performance of peasant agriculture and the macro-economy makes the analysis of reform complex.[11] However, before either current policy reforms can be evaluated or revised packages suggested, gaps in the existing knowledge must be filled. Until now Tanzanian policy-makers have implemented far-reaching interventions in their economy without the benefit of reliable rural socio-economic data. Only by the pains-taking development of an information infrastructure—a process to which our survey is a modest contribution—can policy interventions be improved to achieve the underlying goals of the community.

Notes

1. K. Griffin, 'Institutional change and income distribution in the Chinese countryside', *Oxford Bulletin of Economics and Statistics*, 45, 1983.
2. The United Republic of Tanzania, Ministry of Agriculture, *The Agricultural Policy of Tanzania* (Dar es Salaam, Government Printer, 1983).
3. J. W. Harbeson 'Tanzanian socialism in transition: Agricultural crisis and policy reform', *UFSI Reports* (Hanover, New Hampshire), 30, 1983.
4. World Bank, *Accelerated Development in Sub-Saharan Africa: An Agenda for Action* (Washington DC, World Bank, 1981).
5. International Bank for Reconstruction and Development, *Tanzania: Agricultural Sector Report* (Washington DC, World Bank, 1983).
6. World Bank, op. cit.
7. International Labour Organisation, *Distributional Aspects of Stabilization Programme in Tanzania*, mimeo., (ILO, 1984); and A. Singh, 'The Present Crisis of the World Economy and National and Rural Development in Africa: Analytical and Policy Issues', Paper prepared for the Workshop on Transformation of Agrarian Systems in Centrally-planned Economies of Africa, Arusha, 17–23 Oct., 1983.
8. Harbeson, op. cit.
9. The United Republic of Tanzania, Ministry of Agriculture, op. cit., p. 10.
10. Ibid., pp. 24–5.
11. See D. L. Bevan, A. Bigsten, P. Collier, and J. W. Gunning, *Impediments to Trade Liberalisation in East Africa: the Economics of Rationing* (London, Trade Policy Research Centre, 1986).

Index